# THE
# TRUCK
# DRIVER
# CHRONICLES

VONERIC ABERNATHY

Copyright © 2021 by VonEric Abernathy

All rights reserved. No part of this publication may be reproduced, distributed, or transmitted in any form or by any means, including photocopying, recording, or other electronic or mechanical methods, without the prior written permission of the publisher, except in the case of brief quotations embodied in critical reviews and certain other noncommercial uses permitted by copyright law.

For permission requests, write to the publisher, addressed "Attention: Permissions Coordinator," at the address below.

**ISBN:** 978-1-7346343-7-2

Publishing By:
DemiCo National, LLC
www.DemiCoNational.com

## DEDICATIONS

This book is dedicated to all the unsung heroes past and present that put their lives on the line everyday to deliver products all over the world.
Without truck drivers this world would cease to exist.

We run hard in the rain, sleet, snow, tornadoes, hurricanes, and any type of weather that comes in order to deliver any type of product to make this world a better and more efficient place.

Yet, despite how this world needs truck drivers, truck drivers are one of the most disrespected and under paid industries there is. So, to all the truckers, past and present; thank you for all the hard work that you do.

This is my story.

**TABLE OF CONTENTS**

| | |
|---|---|
| Introduction | 7 |
| 1. The Road Less Traveled | 17 |
| 2. A Student of Life | 29 |
| 3. Withholding Nothing | 45 |
| 4. Enter 2020 | 63 |
| 5. I Love Lucy | 74 |
| 6. Somethings Never Change | 85 |
| 7. Not in the Mood | 103 |
| 8. The Fall of America | 115 |
| 9. The Hitchhiker | 127 |
| 10. Truck and Trailer | 140 |

**INTRODUCTION**

In life, there are roads. There are roads that will take us far from the comfort in which we know, and there are roads that will bring us closer to home than we ever knew possible. There are roads smooth, easy, and accessible, and then there are roads bumpy, broken, and brutal. If you travel long enough, you will find that there are roads scattered with the traveling of others all the same, and then there are the roads quiet, peaceful, and lonely.

I was nearing my 37$^{th}$ year of traveling life's highways when I reached a place within myself in which I found that all the roads I had traveled were all leading me to one precise and clear change of direction. While this change in my life was now occurring in my late 30's, I have to acknowledge that the signs had been present for quite some time.

I had spent most of my life relatively on the same road. It was the road of expectancy, but was it even my expectancy? All of my goals, ideas, and wants that fueled me to get out of the bed every morning; were they even my expectancies or had I built an entire life wanting what I felt I should want. I have always considered myself to be a traveler in some sorts. Let me explain. I have never had an issue really walking away from people or places of which I no longer felt connected.

I'm not by any means a quitter, but I just never had much tolerance for anything that didn't seem like respect and love. So, when love and respect left, I left. I have no regrets about that. Whether it was a failed relationship, chaotic work environment, or unstable friendship, if I didn't know how to do anything at all, I knew how to throw up the peace sign and hit the road. But it wasn't always the physical road. Sometimes, it was a new emotional or mental road that I needed to travel.

I'm sure some people probably viewed me as a runner, but that's not it. I will fight, stick, and stay through all of the issues that come along with traveling life's roads with a spouse, friends, and family. But, when the road ends, I leave. Granted, there were times that maybe I should have hit the road a lot sooner, but either way; I still hit the road. When I felt the calling from God to preach, I changed roads to accept my purpose. When I married my wife, I changed roads to be a better man. I never had any trouble finding female companionship, but marriage was a different road. Even as a father, I changed the road I was on to travel the road needed.

I would be a very present figure in my children's lives. So, by the time I was in my mid 30s there was absolutely no reason for me to hesitate so much when presented with a new road to travel, but I lingered. Some people fear change, but I embrace change; I always have. I never feared change or the opinion of others. Since childhood, I lived in a space of freedom from the opinions of others. So, after a lifetime of traveling the roads least traveled why in the hell was this new road so difficult for me?

Perhaps I wasn't as confident in myself as I thought. Perhaps I wasn't as strong willed as I thought. Perhaps it wasn't the road itself that I feared, but rather my method of travel that gave me pause. Yes, that is it.

I think that a person's relationship with God is their method of travel throughout life's highways, and my spiritual car seemed fine to me. So, why was God insisting that I upgrade something that worked fine? I had spent my entire life in the church. I began preaching in my late teens and was now years into pastoring another congregation.

Why would a new road appear now? Why this constant urge to do more, be more, and give more? I was happy. Overall life was good, or at minimum; life was tolerable. I was in no ways interested in taking such a detour from the life I had built. Yes, there were complications at home, the church, and even at my other two jobs, but I did what I had always done; I made it work. I just wasn't at all interested in this new road and change God kept flashing towards me like a billboard on the side of the interstate.

The more I ignored the signs, the more signs seemed to appear. The signs of the road ahead were everywhere. However, the more I ignored the coming road, the more I began to see what was happening in my life. I had become so used to only truly changing roads when things didn't honor me, that I did not know how to make a change unless I felt unloved or disrespected.

"God, what is the deal?", I can remember verbally speaking one cold November night as I drove to my night job. I had gotten a job as a security guard sitting in the guard shack at the entrance of a manufacturing plant. By the time I would head to this job every night, I was physically drained. So, I used the car ride time to really pray and talk to God; not just to spend time with God, but to stay awake also.

I found that driving always seemed to put me in such a deep stillness that made hearing God so much easier. By now, I was frustrated with being frustrated. I wanted to do so much for God. I wanted to be so much for God, but nothing quenched the feeling of more. Oh, I had so many visions for ministry and the church. We were a small congregation, but that thrilled me, and I was hopeful. Why would God be drawing me out and away from the purpose He had given me?

That night I made it to work. I parked my tiny Hyundai in the same parking space that I always parked in and made my way to the guard shack. I zipped up my coat as I entered and closed the door behind me. Usually, I would be annoyed by the potato chip crumbs or coke can rings left on the desk, but this night I didn't care. I was exhausted, fully exhausted.

Greg began speaking as he clocked out and handed me the clip board, but I heard nothing he said. I just wanted him to hurry and leave. He left, I sat, closed my eyes, and I exhaled. Earlier that evening I had spent my lunch break on my other job consoling a church member following the death of her husband. I had nothing left to give to anyone on that day. I was empty in every way.

I exhaled again as I heard a loud engine nearing the guard shack. I opened my eyes and there it was. The large freight truck absorbed me. Trucks passed through the guard shack all night. It was normal, but this truck was new, and I felt my life was about to change as it neared. The truck stopped, and I looked up at the driver. I waited for him to look down to me. I continued waiting. The waiting continued and I noticed another truck entering the lot. I was becoming irritated. I reached and knocked on the truck's door. Eventually the man looked down. He quickly dried his eyes and looked down to me. I said nothing. We made eye contact and I signed him in on my clipboard. A woman's voice echoed from the truck. He attempted to lower the volume on the radio, but her screeching voice could not be hidden. I stepped away from the truck, and he continued forth as I could hear him pleading with the woman to allow him to speak to his child. The next truck arrived, and I prepared for a very moody driver as I knew this driver to be. He rolled down his window. I spoke,

"What's good Ced? Man, I'm sorry about the hold up. The guy in front of you was having some type of personal situation going on. Sounds like he was getting it rough from his old lady." I said reaching up.

"Is he new?"

"Seems like it."

"Damn. I hope he knows what he's gotten himself into." Ced spoke. I laughed.

"Man, yall got it easy." I laughed. I waited for him to respond. He said nothing. I documented his time. He spoke.

"It ain't what everybody thinks out here." His words quivered and faded. I felt his emptiness. "We ain't got nobody out here on the road. Nobody. We ain't got family, friends, or nobody. I don't even feel like I have God out here with me most of the time." I prepared to speak, but I was too late. Ced rolled up his window and drove away.

I stood there quietly. I had never seen two men in such pain. I felt their pain. I almost felt as if I now carried it. I quickly shielded my eyes as another truck arrived with its headlights on high beam. The driver quickly rolled down the window and began speaking.

"I'm sorry there, Chief. I didn't realize my high beams were on. I didn't blind you, did I?" He asked. I blinked slowly to focus my eyes and when I opened my eyes, I saw it.

There on the side of the driver's door was a bumper sticker that read, *you can't get to the right place the wrong way.* I stared at the quote. The old man spoke again, "You okay son? I ain't blind you, did I?" He laughed. I looked across the yard at the ocean of trucks driven by men and women we had all forgotten.

"I'm fine," I replied. "I can see."

## CHAPTER ONE

*The Road Less Traveled*

"You done lost your damn mind."

"You're gonna quit the church?"

"Have you lost your mind?" Words of the sort became all so common over the next few months as I prepared to catch my bus to Missouri. I took a deep breath as I waited on my bus to arrive. I kicked my feet up on a suitcase I had owned since I was in the United States Army. Like then, there I was awaiting a bus to take me to a new life and journey of service.

I found it ironic that I was leaving on a cold Sunday afternoon in February. This particular day also happened to be the birthday of my youngest son. I was not at ease about missing my son's birthday, but I knew that my new career path would bring many important days without my presence.

So, I decided that this day would be a learning experience for me. Before heading to the bus stop, I stopped by Stone Brook Church where I pastored. Let me be clear. While I did know that God was calling me to a new career and avenue of ministry, I still struggled to place the new calling with the current position of pastor. Pastoring is in no way a part time job. I in no way was accustomed to being away from a church on Sunday mornings. I had spent my entire life in church on Sundays. The only times I had missed church was back during my days in the military.

As we all often do when we struggle to make sense of change, we try to compromise. So, weeks prior to this day, I informed the congregation at Stone Brook that I would be taking another job that would in return limit my attendance, but not my engagement. They were a small congregation, and perhaps their understanding of my financial situation motivated them to support my decision. They knew that I was working multiple jobs outside of the church, and while the church was not able to consistently provide me the salary we had agreed upon, I still performed as pastor and church musician. Don't get me wrong. In no ways am I complaining. I loved what I did. I felt closer to God by my investment into Stone Brook.

It was my great love for the church that confused me so much when I felt God instructing me that my newest calling would be to serve truckers. I didn't know of any other pastors who had ever managed to be on the road as a trucker and serve a congregation as well. Granted, a few truckers would only drive weekdays to be home on the weekend, but that warranted such a financial loss that it never made sense to me. I had every intention to balance both the church and the new position in trucking, even though I had no idea how it would be possible. Deep down I knew that the compromise to do both was not God's plan. It was my plan. However, where I come from church is as close to God as you can get and nothing else can even compare.

You see, while I still felt this strong urge pulling me away from my role in traditional ministry, I couldn't quite reconcile it just yet. I knew that the new career path as a truck driver would not only provide financial stability that I needed to care for my wife and children, but also, I felt I had an opportunity to minister to a new group of people.

Maybe I was fooling myself into believing God would allow me to do both. Maybe the congregation was fooling themselves into believing I could do both as well. In reality, most people knew that the two roles could not coincide, and because I refused to forfeit the new assignment, new career, and new calling; I was told that I was choosing money over God. I struggled to silence the voices of those around me, but they were unending.

"God ain't tell you to do that!"

"The love of money is the root of all evil" You name it, I heard it. I pressed on anyways to the bus stop. I was exhausted. I had hoped that I would have more energy and spiritual peace on this day, but I did not. I was drained by the lack of support.

I did not want to be frustrated this day, but I was. Truthfully, most people already knew that I was going to do what I wanted to do, however, I did want the understanding and support of others around me.

Perhaps because deep down I was wrestling with the new assignment myself.

As I rested and attempted to calm my nerves, a blessing arrived. I also call that blessing, Elijah. Elijah is my first born. Now a teen who is much taller than me, he had the ability to sooth my soul like no one or nothing else. In walked my son who was more than a son, he was my friend. He was the first evidence of just how much God loved me. I always believed that our children are God's gifts to us to heal us. When God knew that the world needed healing, he sent His own son. So, whenever God knew I needed healing, he would dispatch my children. Of course, as a father, I never let them know when I was not at my spiritual or emotional best, but they still healed me, whether they knew it or not.

"I just wanted to say bye." Elijah said. I made a joke as I often do when I'm in an emotional moment. We both laughed and then it was quiet. In that moment, I knew what I wanted for him had to be shown. There he stood. My proud athlete. He's gonna be the next Kobe Bryant; the next Lebron James. I wanted him to be able to progress through life making all of the decisions that he felt was best for him and his relationship with God. I had always taught him that, so in this moment he taught it back to me. I believe that the confirmation of lessons learned by our children is shown when they recite the lessons back to us when we need it ourselves.

"I love you, Son" I said hugging him.

"I love you too." He said. Then I felt the strength of God that I needed to board this bus with faith, peace, and hope. That is exactly what I did.

The bus ride seemed short, as my anticipation was growing. I felt great about myself and my decisions. I wondered if I should text my wife that I had arrived safely. We were not on good terms and had been separated for some time.

Deep down I still believed a reconciliation was in the cards for us. Unsure if she would ignore this text as she had so many others, I decided not to pollute my day with the disappointment of not getting a reply. I checked into my hotel. Typically, the trucking school would cover all hotel costs, but the guy who would be my roommate had already paid for the room and didn't want me to bunk with him. So, I had to cover the costs of my own room on the first night. That didn't bother me at all.

Nothing was going to trouble me this day. I threw my bags on the extra bed and looked around the room. I knew that the coming cold would be horrific, so I pulled one of the new coats from the bag. I looked around the room, exhaled, and then made my first executive decision. I wanted some ribs and steak.

I stepped from my hotel into the cold. This was definitely not the Alabama cold I was used to, so I cussed. I heard laughter so I looked across the parking lot to see two guys dressed in t-shirts, shorts, and flip flops. They walked towards the hotel. I shook my head.

The next day, class was in session. I was ready. I made myself a promise that at the conclusion of every day, I would make a journal-like entry under the heading of *What I Learned Today*. This wasn't a class requirement, but a self-requirement. I sat there like a kid on his first day of high school, well maybe middle school. I watched as the room slowly filled. Then in walked the same two half-dressed young guys I had seen the night before. I looked down at their feet. We casually greeted one another, and class began.

The instructor wasted no time informing us of the seriousness of being behind the wheel of a machine that managed poorly could lead to countless deaths in a matter of seconds. Even when I thought that he had shared enough about the seriousness of driving safely, he continued. I respected that. We began to learn of the process to come, and much more.

There was much more to this career than putting a key in the switch and starting an engine. I had no idea of the safety protocols, requirements, daily checklist, and more. As detailed as the entire process is one would be shocked to know that any semi-truck accidents occur at all. However, no matter how safe you are, accidents do happen. Even with your greatest certainty that you've done everything right, disaster is still always a possibility.

We all sat quietly. I cleared my mind and allowed his words to go deep within me. I never wanted to be the cause of an accident. The information was a bit daunting and exhausting, but it was very well needed.

Class ended and I was ready for dinner. I headed back to my hotel to change clothes and drop off a few items. I stood at my door as I heard the sound of flip flops again. I knew who it was. I turned to the guys. They were now blue, and they were no longer smiling or laughing. I noticed that one of the young guys wore a Florida t-shirt. I opened my door and entered into my room. I unzipped my duffle bag and pulled the other coat from the bag. I snatched the price tag off the coat and headed out of the room.

"Hey! Hey" I shouted as they scurried across the parking lot. "Hey". I couldn't remember their names. They turned to me. I removed my coat and extended my arms to them as I ran to them. "Here. Take my coats." I said.

"What? Man, we can't do that?" The taller guy said. The other young man reached for a coat.

"Look, it's -10 degrees. I don't want to hear it. It's cold out here, and yall aint gonna make it through the rest of training if yall catch Pneumonia." I said. I thought a laugh might help, so I laughed as if I had made a joke. They smiled. "I'm going to get some ribs. Yall wanna come with me? It's my treat?"

About twenty minutes later they were Caucasian again and no longer blue from the cold as the waitress placed our enormous plates before us.

"They got food like this in Florida?" I laughed.

"I don't think so." Randy said. "I don't know how to say thank you enough."

"Me too. Thank you." Adam added. "We didn't expect it to be this cold but wasn't nothing gonna stop us from getting here." He said eating as if he had not eaten in days. I spoke.

"Sometimes, when the right opportunity comes along, your circumstances don't match. You can miss out on the opportunity waiting for your money to line up or resources to come together or you can just trust God and go for it. He'll always make a way when you step out on faith."

"I like that." Randy said, chewing and nodding. "VonEric, you sound like a preacher."

"I am." I said. They both paused for a second.

"You don't act like a preacher or dress like a preacher."

"What does that mean? What does a preacher look like?" I laughed.

"You have an earring. Ain't that like a sin or something?" Adam asked.

"No, it's, not." I smiled.

"Do we need to call you Rev. VonEric? I don't want to be disrespectful. I always heard it's a sin to not call a pastor by his title."

"Are you serious? Who the hell told you that?" I said. "Man, you can call me VonEric. That's my name. You can call me whatever you want. You can call me anything but the N-word. Cause then I'm gonna beat your ass- in the name of Jesus." We all laughed. The customers and staff began looking at our table. We kept laughing and it felt amazing. We left the restaurant after I convinced them to allow me to give them some cash to help with their stay.

That night I returned to my hotel room. I felt relieved. I looked at my phone. I had no missed calls or texts from anyone from Stone Brook. It felt amazing to be able to see someone in need and immediately help them without having to consult a board of trustees, deacons, or finance leaders. There was a reason that I never felt the freedom to be my most authentic self - inside the walls of a church. I realized in that moment that the type of preacher that the world needed, the church did not want.

"Thank you, God." I said. I opened the notebook on my bed and read the heading, *Day One: What Did I Learn Today.*

## CHAPTER TWO

*A Student of Life*


It was not long before I realized that getting behind the wheel of a semi-truck is not for everyone. The truck is an extremely heavy and large vehicle to bring on the road with small vehicles and even motorcycles, so driving one requires much more adequate training and understanding than that of an ordinary car owner. It cannot be understood overnight. This is why truck driving school is of great importance.

Drivers spend most of their day-to-day time during schooling either in the classroom or on the road. If you cannot sit in the classroom to learn how to drive the truck, you definitely cannot sit in the truck long enough to make the sometimes long and tedious deliveries. We learned so much that never even crossed my mind. We learned things like the pre-trip inspection procedure, logbook keeping, and federal motor carrier regulations. Now I don't want you to feel as if you are in trucking school just by reading this story, but I do want you to share in this experience with me.

There is so much more to driving a truck than simply sitting behind the wheel and footing a couple of pedals. We had to learn how to be safe drivers, which includes looking out for smaller vehicles and motorcycles, obeying the speed limits and other traffic laws, and we learned how to operate the truck safely so that we can be safe on the road.

Pre-trip inspections are very important even though I had no idea what they were. We learned the importance of inspecting the vehicle before getting on the road every single time you drive it. If you don't slowly and carefully inspect the truck and something goes wrong, you could end up killing someone. Of course, I don't want something like that on my conscience the rest of my life. It is the law in most if not all states that you fill out your logbook accurately and keep it up to date within the past four hours. I had to study the correct way to fill out your logbook so I would always avoid trouble with the law as I travel state to state.

Mounting your trailer to your rig and unhooking it again is something drivers do thousands of times over the course of their careers but getting the hang of it originally can be hell for some.

As you might have imagined, on the road is where the real training begins. Whether it's on a 22-foot conventional or a 48- and 53-foot trailer, drivers are out on the highway within the first few weeks, in order to get them quickly used to being behind the wheel of a semi. I was learning everything. Much like driver's education class in high school, we were taken on highways first, and then we were put in complicated or unconventional driving scenarios.

Tony, the lead instructor informed us that sometimes, you'll find yourself in tight situations.

"We'll teach you how to maneuver in small towns, squeeze between tight buildings, drive down alleyways, make it around traffic circles, and even backing up your truck and trailer without jackknifing." He explained.

I started feeling that I had been in church too long when every word spoken gave me sermon ideas. *Focus VonEric*. I told myself.

I could have not been more pleased with my teachers. You have to understand. I had a very difficult experience with my high school teachers, so to have an instructor that is determined to help the students was refreshing to me. Granted, I was now a fully grown man seeking employment, but any questions that I had I felt were answered clearly. Sometimes in life you don't realize how deeply some things hurt you until you actually find yourself in similar situations. Well, trucking school forced me to stare eye to eye with past hurts and pains I had from my high school days that I had never healed.

During my teens I found myself at the mercy of a difficult teacher. She was not difficult because she wanted to pull the best student out of me. She was difficult because I was black, and even she was black. I don't know if she felt she had an obligation to be harder on the black kids for our own good, or if she struggled with self-hatred. Whatever, her reasons were, she scared me. There was never much help that came from Mrs. Rhodes. She would stop or even backtrack when the white students presented a question, but when the black children asked; we were criticized for not paying attention. We were told to find the answer on our own. We were shamed.

"Look it up! Read it yourself!" She would snap at me almost daily. With her hand on her hip, she would always respond to my questions with," Ignorance is bliss." Eventually I would just stop asking questions.

Luck or God would have it that decades later I would be a pastor who often visited the church where her son pastored. So, one particular Sunday I saw her in the congregation. Now, a grown man I almost felt intimidated to speak, preach, or represent God because of her. I refused to allow her to have power over me. I had seen her at another church years before and she wasted no time criticizing my clothes, posture, earring, and whatever else she could think of.

"Preachers don't do this. Preachers don't do that. Preachers. Preachers" Mrs. Rhodes never missed an opportunity to critique me on the ways she thought

I wasn't enough. She had bullied me since I was a kid, and I could not let her take my voice from God from me. I made my way to the podium and spoke. I acknowledged her as my former educator. She blushed and smiled foolishly as the congregation applauded her. Her smile quickly faded as I recited all her abusive words that would always ring in my ears from my time as her student.

Maybe that wasn't the proper moment or setting, but it was the moment I chose. I had been invited to speak by Mrs. Rhodes' son on Teacher's Appreciation Day, so I spoke. The only thing that would have made that service any better would be if Mrs. Rachel had of been in the congregation too. I could have killed two birds with one stone. Let me explain. Again, there I was a teen and I had found myself at the mercy of another black adult who had a reputation among students, parents, and even faculty of being unfair to black students.

Mrs. Rachel was the popular youthful guidance counselor, and all the black upperclassmen would always warn the black freshmen to avoid her. Well, circumstance would have it that I could not avoid her. So, I often found myself in her office. Whether it was for ACT preparation, an altercation with another student, or college plans, she was the counselor assigned to my class. I knew that she did not like me. She looked at me as if I was beneath her. She looked at me as if I were an embarrassment. One afternoon I waited in the lobby outside of her office with other students as we all prepared to speak to her of future plans and more.

    I listened to her give the students confidence, surety, and support in pursuing their higher education. Having received very high marks on my ACT, I was confident she would not only be proud of me but help direct me towards a path of greatness.

    "The army?" I asked looking at the pamphlet she tossed across the desk to me. I didn't lift the pamphlet from the table.

    "The United States National Guard." She said directly.

    "I don't think…."

"You need discipline." She interrupted. I heard the voices of the other students outside the door. I wondered why she felt the only black kid in the group needed discipline. Some of the students had been problematic students since the start of the year.

"VonEric, listen to me." She said realizing that I knew she had not spoken anything of the sort to anyone else but me. "I'm trying to help you, and you need to be disciplined. The military can discipline you." I felt like I would scream if she used that word again. There was a silence. I felt all of my energy fading. "What's it gonna be? I have other students waiting on me." She said. I exhaled and reached for the pamphlet.

I graduated from trucking school, and the next step was training. I would undergo three weeks of driving with a trainer accompanying me. The trainers were typically men or women who had extensive experience in trucking. Do you have patience with others? Are you able to communicate in detail? Can you give constructive criticism? Do you have established knowledge of what you will be training?

These are the questions that trainers are typically asked by trucking companies before they assign new drivers to trainers. However, the guy with the questionnaire must have been off work the week they approved George Lee. I was a little uneasy about having someone else in such a small space with me for so long, but by this time I was a little lonely. It might be a new opportunity to make a new friend.

I knew from the first moment I sat in the truck with George Lee that we would have complications. I am a sociable person, and while I'm not expecting us to be best pals, we are about to spend the next three weeks almost shoulder to shoulder. George Lee was perhaps old enough to be my grandfather, and made it abundantly clear from the start that he had no interest in casual talk, friendship, or even kindness for that matter. At first, I thought he was someone who simply took his job too seriously, but then it began to be more difficult.

"You need to get this right. You ain't gone' mess this up for me." He would snap. "I ain't gone show you nothing. You gone get it or you ain't. Yall always trying to get the easy way out."

"Wait. You're not about to just be speaking to me however you want. I understand I need to learn, but I'm not your child." I said as I put the truck in park. I looked at him. He pretended to be making notes on his clipboard. "Furthermore, who is yall?" I asked.

George Lee didn't reply, but I had experienced this before, so I knew what I was experiencing. George Lee, like many other blacks I had encountered had acquired a position in life that he felt he had to strive to accomplish. I salute that. However, something inside of him likely told him that he was undeserving of the position because he was black. Apparently, for him to have the position meant he was extremely lucky and should not screw it up. So, any other black person who came along George Lee felt as if they were almost a risk of his success or as if every black person represented him. He seemed nervous that he was even assigned to train a black man. He felt as if I was trying to cut corners figuratively and literally.

George Lee reminded me of a few deacons of Stone Brook who I knew never liked me much less respected me. They too just saw me as some kid with an undeserving position that they were forced to work with. Well, I guess they had grown weary of attempting to work with me just as much as I had grown weary of the same.

By this time, I had resigned as pastor of Stone Brook. I began avoiding phone calls from family attempting to pressure me back into a world of what they believed to be the only road map to God. While normally I may have had the emotional endurance to tolerate George Lee, but at this time I did not. He reminded me too much of people who always made me feel that I was not enough.

I felt so tense around him. I felt as if he wanted me to fail. I finally requested a new trainer. Within a couple of days, I was paired with my new trainer. Immediately, we clicked. I became excited, thrilled, and even honored. I felt as if I was becoming one with the truck and the power it held.

Joe applauded me when he felt it was deserving, and he critiqued me when he felt it was deserving. I appreciated. Whether you're training someone to drive a big rig or spiritually training someone to align with God, it is important to train them with honesty, open mindedness, and truth, not preference. Spiritually, I was now learning the difference between God's expectations and the religious preferences of denominations I had spent my whole life thinking was God's request. While Joe trained me on how to safely navigate the highway in the big rig, I trained him on how to navigate life's highways in the human experience. Surprisingly, the fundamentals were not so different.

Do your daily checklist before you get started, confirm your destination, and don't get distracted by the other drivers on the road with you. I always enjoyed healthy conversation.

"Don't let it get to you. It comes with the job." Joe said after we both listened to a racist comment from the CB radio as we journeyed through Georgia.

"Breaker Breaker this is Bobby's World, Yall be watchful of a family of monkeys and baby gorillas on the off ramp at exit 354. They're having car trouble. I might throw them a few bananas or a job application." The raspy old voice laughed. I didn't say anything. I held my composure as we neared exit 354. I slowed as a tow truck had just arrived to help the young black woman and her children. We arrived at a truck stop.

After we would make our deliveries for the day, we'd head to bed. We didn't have far to go because the bunk beds were behind our seats in the truck's cab. I regularly asked Joe which bunk he wanted even though I knew that trainers always got the bottom bunk. It isn't allowed to offer gifts, money, or anything of the sort to your trainers, but I wanted to honor him in whatever way possible to let him know that I appreciate him. He made his way to the bottom bunk.

"You want anything out the store? A drink? Chips?" I asked.

"No, I'm good. Just look out for those lizards." He said getting comfortable.

"Lizards?" I asked looking out the truck window to the ground. "What lizards?"

"The Lot Lizards." He replied.

"What the hell is a Lot Lizard?"

"Ain't nobody told you about the Lot Lizards?"

"Nope. Nobody." I said. He leaned down and pointed out the passenger window. I looked to see a woman in a very short skirt climbing into a truck as the driver reached for her hand. Another woman with a blonde Marilyn Monroe wig, waived her arms in the air to a truck that had just arrived. I waited for someone to obtain her, and I exited the truck for the store. I tried to hurry through the parking lot avoiding any hidden Lot Lizards.

"Dahling, you are something else! My goodness! I say you rocked this old man's world." I heard as a truck's passenger door opened. I knelt between the trucks. I was in no mood to deal with this foolishness. "You got a number? I make rounds to these parks twice a month." The voice said. I recognized the voice. I looked at the truck next to me. A bumper sticker was on the driver's door. A few seconds later I saw tennis shoes hit the pavement and the passenger door to the truck closed. I watched as a young black man walked from the truck. He pulled baby wipes from his backpack and began scrubbing his lips and tongue as he walked towards the store. I glanced back at the bumper sticker that read, *Bobby's World*. I walked towards the store. I entered and made my way to the bathroom. The young man was at the sink. He had scattered the contents of his backpack across the filthy countertop. I used the urinal as I heard him counting to ten. Ten. For ten dollars he gave himself to a racist animal. My heart broke. He couldn't have been but perhaps 20 years old. I washed my hands.

"What's up? How are you?" I asked without looking at him in the mirror. He did not respond. He reminded me of Mrs. Reilly's son. Mrs. Reilly was a church member of Stone Brook who struggled to come to terms with her son's sexuality. No matter how much I instructed her to love and him, she refused to budge on what she believed to be the greatest sin. Her son Kenny had run away from home, and we had no idea of where he had gone. She did not seem to care, but I cared. How could I not care? How could anyone not care?

I dried my hands and left the bathroom as the young man began brushing his teeth. I knew that by this time he had begun to cry. I placed my few items on the counter before the cashier.

"Is this it?" She asked.

"Can you add a chicken tender dinner, please?"

"You want honey mustard sauce or ranch?" She asked.

"Ask the young black guy that comes out of the bathroom. It's for him." I said reaching for my wallet. She looked at me as if I had been one of the drivers to have sex with one of the Lot Lizards on that night, but you know what? I didn't care. I didn't care what she thought of me or my reason for helping someone in need, and it felt great.

"Keep the change." I said as I grabbed my items. I walked from the store.

## CHAPTER THREE

*Withholding Nothing*

"Dammit! Shit!" I cannot believe this. "Really? Ain't this a bitch!" Now, before you start in on judging me with the list of things preachers don't do or say, I'm sure you've understood by now that I am not by any means perfect. Put yourself in my situation. There I was perhaps the most focused, dedicated, and disciplined driver in my class, and what happens on my first day of solo driving? I hit a pedestrian!

Well, I didn't actually hit a pedestrian. I hit a pedestrian sign, but dammit it felt like I had hit an actual person. According to everyone around me, I acted like I had hit a pedestrian instead of a pedestrian sign. This was my first day. So, I continued cussing as I jumped down from the truck to see the sign that was no more. I stared at the sign and for a moment wondered if it were a bigger sign. Perhaps a sign from God? Isn't it amazing that no matter how much success we have that sometimes the slightest slip ups can cause us to doubt ourselves? Well, let me add a bit more context.

I was now months into my new career, and I was happy to be released on the road on my own. Joe had done a great job of training me, so I was ready. I couldn't allow this mistake to be any more than just a mistake, but it was difficult. It was difficult for me to have to explain how I made such a preventable error. A preventable accident is what it was referred to when I had to go and see the safety manager. I felt ashamed. I paid a citation for the sign, and I moved on back to the truck.

You may hear a story such as that and not think much of it, but the moment was major for me. The realization that the moment was so major for me also sent me into a mental drift of why it was so important to me. It didn't take me long to process my experience. My phone had long stopped ringing from friends, family, and anyone from Stone Brook. I was now alone, and I knew I was alone.

Even the fellow clergy that I once referred to as my brothers in the gospel vanished. I found myself overcompensating by the feeling of being exiled and thrown away, by aiming to be the best driver that I could be. When I hit the pedestrian sign on the first day, I felt failure. Most of all, I heard voices of inadequacy. But I knew that the voices were not mine. The voices belonged to the people I had spent so many years around who only knew religion, not God. As I climbed back into my new truck and buckled my seat belt, I gave myself one of the best gifts that I could have ever given myself.

I've never been a materialistic guy by any means. Money, cars, clothes, and jewelry really mean nothing to me. I've never felt as if my identity was linked to my possessions, so I had to gift myself something on that day that wouldn't serve my ego, but my soul. The gift that I gave to myself before I started the engine, was the gift of imperfection. I had to give myself permission to be the flawed, sometimes impatient, and overly zealous man that I was. I had to give myself permission to be me and to know that God was perfectly cool with me. I let that gift enter my soul. I started the engine, and my journey began.

I loved every moment of the highway. I was getting used to everything. Even though I struggled with back pain, I knew that it would be temporary. Even if not, it would not stop me. My first day turned into my first month, six months, and so forth. Time was flying by, and I found myself talking more to God while driving than I had ever done so before in my life.

I would find myself talking to God as if He were in the passenger seat. I loved every moment. There was never really a plan to talk to Him, it was just something about being on the road alone and seeing all that He had made that brought my mouth to utter words to Him. From the mountains to the rivers, lakes, and countrysides, I knew that He had masterfully created it all just as He had created me. It felt amazing.

When I wasn't speaking to God, I would find myself listening to audiobooks, podcasts, and discussions about religion and politics. After a while, I had a break and I decided to take a trip home. I wasn't really sure of what to expect as I was quite a different man by this time. Contact with my wife was very minimum so I knew that my visit would consist of a hotel room. I returned home and visited with family. I gave financial assistance to those who needed help, and I even visited a local church. I sat in the sanctuary of the church and while everyone else shouted, celebrated, and danced all around me; I almost felt numb. I did feel numb. I had become so accustomed to such soul fueling encounters with God and everyday folks on the road, that listening to a choir sing the same songs they've sang for the last 30 years did nothing for me.

I don't know if the look on my face indicated that I wasn't spiritually fed by the service or if it was rumors of me now being a sinner. However, several people sacrificed their Sunday afternoon time and began telling me just how wrong I was for no longer serving as pastor.

I just decided to take it all in with a grain of salt, but it was not easy. No one wanted to hear of my new experiences. No one cared, because I had come from an entire culture of people who only know God to be one thing. So, their lack of imagination was not an insult to me. It was an insult to God, and I couldn't allow myself to take it personally. Even if I did want to say,

"Get the hell out of my face."

I saw my children, and before long I was leaving out on the road again. On my way out of North Alabama, I drove down Highway 20. When I came to the intersection where I could see Stone Brook, I felt a pain in my heart. I exhaled it away and continued driving.

I drove on to Birmingham to pick up a load. I then took that load to Michigan. I left Michigan and picked up another load in West Virginia, before I headed to New Orleans. I left The Big Easy just before a hurricane threat and made it to Houston. I have to admit, I was loving the opportunity to eat foods from so many different places. Granted, it wasn't as if I could just pull my truck through a drive thru, but I managed to walk around the cities during the time remaining before my next assignment.

After Houston, I journeyed the highways to Indiana again. I was making phenomenal timing, so I arrived in Indianapolis on a Sunday night. I was not expected to pick up my next load until the next morning. I decided that I would just chill at the truck stop and relax. My truck was fully equipped with a tv, microwave, minifridge, hot plate, and bunk beds. What more could I want? Still wrestling with now very intense back pain, I decided to go into the truck stop for a pain reliever and a hot shower. I was now fearing a damaged nerve or disc in my back, but I trusted that God would heal me. He had to heal me. I could not forfeit my job so early into the career. Something had to happen, and I needed help. I was in constant agonizing pain.

I made my way into the country truck stop and I waited on a shower to become available. I looked at the high-priced aspirin and shook my head. I was down to my last ten dollars. Could I spend three dollars on aspirin? I began to focus in on the sounds and banter of truckers. Now, contrary to the type of truckers that are depicted on television and in movies, truckers aren't sitting around dipping snuff and cussing all day long. I cussed long before I became a trucker thank you very much.

The banter and conversation that I knew was from a group of truckers, was simply laughter. As a trucker, we spend our entire lives on the roads and send out monies back home. When we receive good news, we are alone. When we receive bad news, we are alone. So, the family of truck drivers is a group of men and women too who seek relationships and genuine human interaction. I followed the sounds of the crowd and the closer I got to the rear of the truck stop the more I realized that what I had walked into. The moment my feet hit the doorway opening, I heard the words and music.

"We need a sermon! We need a word." The room was electrifying. I had walked into a worship service in the rear of the truck stop. I felt God standing next to me, and apparently, He started using me as a magnet to their eyes because within a few seconds every eye in the room was on me.

There I stood, clearly in a moment orchestrated by God. What would I preach? What would I say? Would I say anything? My Bible was in the truck. God and I both knew that I would preach because I love preaching, so I told myself to shut up. I placed my duffle bag near the old jukebox. The crowd began applauding as I walked to the podium. I don't want you to misunderstand what I am explaining. I was not excited by their applause. I was excited and somewhat emotional to have been welcomed and received by complete strangers more than people who had known of my ministry since I was in my late teens.

There I was in Indiana. We were all truckers from God knows where. I didn't know them, and they didn't know me. They didn't know one another. There was no investigation to determine my denomination or their denominations. It was just the belief that God is one and we were all one. I was at peace.

"Let us not be weary in well-doing; for in due season, we shall reap if we faint not." I said.

"Alright brother."

"Praise God brother."

"Look at someone near to you." I said. "Look them in the eye as if their life depended on them believing your words." I instructed. They all did as I asked. "Tell them, don't give up.". I said as I looked into the eyes of a man leaning against the trash can. He had the name Gerald embroidered on his shirt. A few seconds later the room was silent. The applauds and praises had stopped. Most smiles were gone, and the energy had changed. It wasn't as if God had left the room, it was much different than that. In fact, it was actually the opposite. It was as if God's presence had increased in such a way that it forced us all to sit in our own hurt, pain, loneliness, frustration, bitterness, and despair. I felt their pain. All twenty-nine of them, I felt their pain, especially Gerald's. I closed my eyes and asked God for strength. What had I just walked into?

This was not the type of congregation I was used to preaching to. These were people who knew where they rested in their soul. Like me, they knew that they needed God, and they were not ashamed to own it. The room felt heavy, and the silence seemed to last forever as I continued looking across the room. God wouldn't release me to speak. I could just look, but as I looked one by one, I saw. I saw what God saw. He allowed me to see pain. I exhaled as they made eye contact with me. I felt my phone vibrating in my pocket. I ignored it.

I found myself looking at God's children in their most raw and natural humanity, and I felt compassion. I felt heavy, but it was an honor to feel the heaviness of the crowd. I knew that they needed something and at that time, God had trusted me to fulfill those needs. I spoke.

"Every day each of us encounter thoughts that don't belong to us. As I'm hooking up a trailer, I hear those thoughts. As I am driving, I hear those thoughts. It is a fight every day to fight the thoughts that aren't even mine. Every day we all fight thoughts that are telling us to give up in one way or another."

"Amen." A voice echoed from the back of the room. I continued.

"You're getting too old to be out on this road. You're too young to be out on this road. Your family doesn't miss you. Your family doesn't love you. They're just waiting for you to send your paycheck back home. God doesn't love you. And then there is the one that really hurts, you don't love God." I said. "I know I'm not the only one who gets sick of the thoughts that don't belong to me."

"You're not the only one brother."

"You're not alone brother. It's hell out here by yourself." An older black man said clapping his hands together. I spoke.

"I want each one of you to know that it is time for you to rise up and tell those thoughts that they are not your thoughts. They are not thoughts of God. You are loved. I am loved. God loves me, and I love God. I don't care if I don't set foot in a church again, I love God and God loves me. I don't care if I'm working on Sunday mornings for the rest of my life, I love God and God loves me. Do you know how I know God loves me?" I asked the crowd as I felt my hands tingling.

"How preacher?"

"Tell us how you know preacher?"

"I said do you know how I know God loves me?" I repeated. "I know God loves me because He won't let me give up. Even when I want to throw in the towel, He not only walks with me and talks with me, but He rides with me! He drives with me when I'm alone and no one seems to care about me." I felt myself jumping. When I returned to myself, the crowd worshipped and wept. The pain in my back was gone.

Before I could focus my eyes on the room behind my tears, I felt arms wrapping around me and hands patting my back. I felt love, and I knew it was God. I knew that everything about the moment was God. The weary man by the trash can clenched his fist together near his face as tears fell from his eyes. We made eye contact. His hurt ran deep, and I saw it. He knew that I saw it. He turned and walked from the room. I felt my phone vibrating again in my pocket.

I grabbed my duffle bag and prepared to follow him when the trucker who later identified himself as Big E, grabbed my shoulder.

"Hold up Rev. We need to take up a collection." Big E said.

"No, that's okay. I don't need that."

"We have to be obedient to God just like you do." He said removing his baseball cap from his head. He began passing his cap around the room. Within a matter of seconds, his cap was full. Another trucker removed his cap and collected more offerings until his cap was full. This continued and on until it seemed as if no one was wearing headgear anymore. A few minutes later, Big E gathered all the cash together and placed it in a white paper bag he had gotten from the cashier at the front of the truck stop. He folded the bag as much as possible as he leaned into my ear.

"Because of you, I'm gonna keep on a little bit further. I can't promise that I'll run on to the end, but because of that word, I promised the good Lord that I'll run on another day." He said as his tears soaked the bag. "This isn't much, but this is a little over five grand. Bless you my brother for letting us know God hadn't forgotten about us." He said. I placed the money in the bottom of my duffle bag and made my way from the room.

Ten dollars is what I had in my pocket less than an hour before as I stood before the medicine aisle shaking my head at the bottle of aspirin that I could not afford. I made my way to the coffee machine. I saw the troubled man who had caught my attention preparing to exit the store.

"Have a good evening brother." I said loudly. He turned to me. He continued weeping. This was not a typical pain, and I knew it. His pain was much different than anything else I had felt that night. I sat my cup down on the counter and made my way to him. I prepared to speak, but he spoke first.

"Can I bother you for a cup of coffee?" He asked. I knew that he needed more than a cup of coffee. He knew that I knew that also. So, he spoke again. "I've been here for a few days now. I'm sorry, I'm Gerald."

"This truck stop?" I asked.

"Yea."

"Are you over your mileage?" I asked. Due to safety protocols drivers are typically allowed to only drive 70 hours a week or 11 hours a day. Once we reach those hours, we are required to sit for 34 hours until a new clock begins.

"I ain't got a truck here." He said.

"Oh. I assumed you were a trucker like the rest of us back there." I said reading the name of the trucking company on his cap.

"I am a trucker. I was driving with my partner and I had to go home to take care of some…." His voice got weak and he hesitated. "She was just a kid. She was just a kid." He began to crumble. "I had to go home to bury my daughter. It took everything I had to go home, cover her burial, and get back here to Indiana where I was supposed to meet my partner. He hasn't shown up, and I don't think he will now. I think I'm out of a job now."

"Man, I'm sorry."

"I just want a cup of coffee. I'm tired. Man, I'm tired. I'm tired. I'm so tired. That was my daughter!" He shouted as his voice echoed throughout the store.

"I want to help you." I said.

"Preacher, I don't need nothing. I don't want nothing but coffee. That's it. I ain't got nothing else. I just want a coffee."

"Brother, you listen to me. Look at me. LOOK AT ME!" I shouted. We locked eyes. "He's bigger than that! You're bigger than that! He's more than a cup of coffee. He loves you more than that." Realizing that I was only seconds from crying, I turned and walked away.

I cried not only for his pain, but for God's grace. I was happy, and I knew I was His. As I made my way to the glass door, I saw the reflection of Gerald's face as he opened the white paper bag I had placed in his hands.

"Wait! Preacher! Wait! No! Take this! I can't accept this."

"Go home to your family Gerald." I said as I continued walking. "God is with you. He's got you. He's got you." I walked out of the store and began making my way to my truck that was now my home in every sense of the word. I exhaled heavily. I pulled my phone from my back pocket. I noticed the several missed calls. I dialed the number.

"Yes. This is VonEric. I missed a few calls from this number."

"Hello, Mr. Abernathy. This is John Haines." The man on the phone said. "I have been trying to reach you.

"What can I do for you Mr. Haines?" I felt uneasy.

"You should have received an email from me within the recent days. I just wanted to confirm that you did receive the email."

"Who is this again?" I asked looking around.

"John Haines. Attorney John Haines."

"Attorney?" I said. "Who's attorney?"

"I assume that you did not receive my emails. Mr. Abernathy, I represent your wife. I am reaching out to you to discuss obtaining your signature." He explained.

"My signature? What are you…"

"She has filed for divorce, and we need you to sign the divorce papers." He blurted. I looked back to the truck stop entrance as Big E waved farewell to me.

"Have a good one Preacher. God bless you brother." Big E shouted as he vanished.

"Mr. Abernathy, are you there?" John said.

"Fine. Fuck it. Send me the papers."

## CHAPTER FOUR

*Enter 2020*

After signing my divorce papers, I gained a new perspective on relationships also. By this time, 2020 had arrived and the new year brought about new excitements and new frustrations. Before I resigned from Stone Brook, I unintentionally angered many church members as I barred the discussions of politics at the church.

Being that we were an all-black southern Baptist church, of course the congregation was predominantly liberal. For the recent years it seemed as if the political and racial tensions across the country would become the subject of messages and comments at Stone Brook. So, I stood against such. Even though I knew which direction the majority of the congregants leaned politically, I still in no way felt that a church should use its platform to discredit or challenge those of opposing political views. I had my own views of

Donald Trump, and they were strong views, however my views had no place in the pulpit. I wanted everyone to feel spiritually safe at Stone Brook. Even though I failed to do so, it was my intention to establish a political free space. The world was divisive enough. I wanted to establish a safe space.

Here I was now a truck driver, and shortly after the new year arrived my company began establishing clear and direct boundaries when it came to politics. I loved it. I would listen to my favorite podcast while on the road, or even discuss my thoughts with friends who I might share conversation with from back home. I avoided discussing the upcoming political nightmare with those around me in the trucking industry. We had enough to focus on. I was getting more work than ever before. Several drivers found themselves hit hard with the flu of some sort, which meant the remaining drivers had to cover their loads.

On January $26^{th}$, the death of Kobe Bryant impacted many drivers in ways that is still difficult to explain. I was somewhere between Texas and Oklahoma when I heard the news. I had just pulled up at a Bucker Bill's Truck Stop. The second I turned off my engine and opened my door, the driver next to me began shouting from his truck to me.

"Man, we done lost a legend."

"Say what?"

"A legend." He repeated. I jumped down to the ground as did he. He met me in front of his truck. He looked at me. "You don't know do you? You haven't heard."

"Heard what?" I asked almost becoming irritated.

"Brother, Kobe Bryant's helicopter went down this afternoon. He's dead."

"What? Damn." I said as we continued forth in the store. By the time we entered the store I watched as people huddled around staring up at the television in the corner. The crowd was relatively quiet as the reporter speculated the other people who were possibly on the helicopter with Kobe. I grabbed a cup of coffee and sat.

"That fella was one of the good ones, and I don't mean just at playing ball." An older gentleman said to me. I nodded.

"Yea. I'm not a big basketball fan, but I've always heard good things about him. He did a lot of good for a lot of people." I agreed.

"That's right. They're saying he was transporting a bunch of kids to basketball practice when his chopper went down." The old man shook his head. I turned to look back at the tv. Kobe's impact on the world was evident in that moment. I went to the restroom, and by the time I returned the energy in the room had changed.

The grief and devastation could be cut with a knife. Shock and a stunned silence washed over the truck stop on this Sunday afternoon as the tragic news spread that Kobe Bryant and his 13-year old daughter both died in the helicopter crash. Beyond the truck stop, athletes and fans, politicians and celebrities alike struggled to process the death of an athletic icon.

"I don't see what the fuss is." A voice said from the front of the store. Many faces turned to see the overweight man that was speaking. "He was a fucking rapist. I'm glad he's gone." The man said before heading to the restrooms. I felt a pain in my heart, and I then returned to my truck. I was not a big fan of Kobe Bryant, but something about his life and death was impacting me in a way that I needed to be alone so that I could process.

As the day continued on, every news outlet covered nothing but Kobe. The few outlets that had mentioned this mystery illness spreading across Europe had even turned their focus to covering the death of the legendary athlete. It had been such a long time that our deeply divided nation shared a common interest or loss. Magic Johnson was in tears, Michael Jordan was in shock, and the sports world was in mourning. Tributes poured in from all corners of the globe, celebrating and remembering one of the incredible playing careers and most legendary athletes.

Like so many of the greats stars of the NBA, Magic, Tiger, Jordan — the world knew him by one name, Kobe — or *"Mamba"* to many. Adding to the devastation of the tragedy was the death of his daughter, Gianna. Kobe had retired from playing himself, but his daughter would be his protégé. She kept him close to the sport, and the father and daughter were reportedly flying to one of her games Sunday when the crash occurred. The moment first seemed real to me when President Barak Obama expressed his condolences to Kobe's wife Vanessa. I read the tweet from my truck. Just like everything else he'd done, Trump soon followed Obama.

Trump called the death of the Lakers superstar "terrible news" in a tweet. It became clear in that moment just how unliked Trump was when people were even angered for him to express condolences to someone as loved as Kobe. Truthfully, Trump had a tendency to always say the wrong thing so when he began to speak on Kobe everyone tensed up hoping he wouldn't say something befitting of typical Trumpisms. Joe Biden even expressed condolences as did world leaders from around the globe.

As I continued on traveling city to city, the love of Kobe was depicted with billboards, posters, vigils, and more. It was a nationwide-worldwide loss, and I was seeing the pain. Truckers began wearing Kobe caps, shirts, and even jerseys.

While the love was clear, the hatred towards Kobe was evident as well. I realized that I couldn't even mention the tragedy of Kobe's death to many truckers without them bringing up the 2004 rape accusations against him.

"You're supposed to be a preacher. How can you sit here and show remorse for a rapist?" I was asked at a loading dock in Pennsylvania. Kelly folded her arms at me as I signed the papers before me. I hated that I had even made an effort to engage in small talk. She knew me from my regular runs to this company. While our exchanges had always been friendly in the past, she was clearly frustrated now.

"Were you in that hotel room? I know I wasn't." I replied while signing.

"I didn't have to be in that room. I know a rapist when I see a rapist." She said. I looked at the *Make America Great Again* coffee mug in her hand. I tried my best to shut the hell up, but I think you have an idea of how that went.

"You do know that the man who came up with that slogan on your coffee mug has been accused of rape by a couple dozen of women, right?" I said placing my pen on the countertop.

"Do you know how much money Trump has? Why would he need to rape any woman? He can get any woman that he wants!" She said placing her hands on her hip.

"Trump can get any woman that he wants? Donald J. Trump?"

"Yes. Do you know how rich he is?" She said.

"Kelly, aside from the fact that you're implying that any woman will have sex with Trump for the right price tag, Kobe was rich also. I'm just saying that it is a tragedy. Aside from everything, he still did a lot to help people. Who am I to judge? Who are you to judge?"

"I don't care how much good he did. It doesn't erase rape."

"I never said it did, but we don't know what happened in that room. The case was dropped, and you can't even let the man be honored in his death without feeling the need to attack him."

"I ain't got to honor somebody like him. I'm a real Christian. I disagree PREACHER." She said sarcastically. I stared at her.

"You know that doesn't work with me, right? I asked.

"What?"

"That."

"What?" She asked louder.

"That! You can't offend me or shame me if I don't fit what you believe a preacher to be. I'm not called to meet your approval. To be honest, I really don't give a fuck what you think. I was just trying to make small talk and be polite with you. Now, have a blessed day." I said as I walked away.

I know. I know, but dammit; I needed that moment. It was clear to me then what was so painful to me personally about the death of Kobe Bryant. Aside from the tragedy at hand, his life was a tragedy. I don't know if the accusations against him were true or not, but people were determined to remember him only as what they knew him to be when they felt like he disappointed them. That pissed me off because that was my experience as well. Granted, I had not been accused of rape or anything remotely close. I was accused of what church folks called *back sliding* simply because I took a different road to ministry.

What if I spent my entire life doing good and making a difference to only be remembered for rumors and accusations against me? I made my way back to my truck. I was frustrated. I realized that I had again encountered the type of Christian that triggered the worst in me.

There are so many self-proclaimed Christians who are self-righteous, judgmental, and have hearts of stone. It amazes me how much they manage to fuck up God's one requirement, love. Everything comes full circle to love, and I did not understand how anyone could not find compassion for the tragedy that had fallen upon the Bryant family. I hated the idea of sharing a religion with people who acted like Kelly. I started the engine and continued on to pick up my next load.

I was not surprised when my conviction started kicking in a few weeks later about how I had spoken to Kelly. A month passed as I prepared to return to her company. I knew that I would apologize for my harsh words. Judgmental Christians had the ability to trigger me like nothing else, and I needed to heal from that. I knew it. As I returned, I noticed fewer trucks in the yard. Something was different. I arrived at the gate. Out walked a man with a clip board to record my time and that was the first time that I saw it. I looked at him as he pulled a medical or doctor's mask over his face. I looked around and saw a few other people also wearing masks.

"What the hell? What the hell is going on?"

# CHAPTER FIVE

*I Love Lucy*

No one in the world, especially the trucking industry could have imagined the unforeseen disaster that was happening upon the U.S. as Covid-19 showed its head. With a worldwide death toll of more than 200 and more than 9,800 cases, the World Health Organization declared a public health emergency on January 31st, 2020. Person to person contact was now spreading the virus across the globe and Covid-19 had made its way to America.

We didn't know what to think at first, especially after global flights were being stopped and restricted. The paranoia began to increase as more and more cases began to plague Americans. Some trucking companies were already taking measures to limit the spread even though there was no clear course of action known yet on how to prevent the spread.

Originally, many truckers like most people did not take the virus seriously. Talks of the Kobe Bryant tragedy were immediately halted by now fears of this mysterious virus.

"Hello?" I answered my phone as a family member called. I continued driving as I listened to her voice over the Bluetooth system.

"VonEric, where are you?" She asked.

"I'm in Georgia right now. What's up?"

"What do you plan on doing about the virus? They say its getting bad and its spreading fast." She sounded concerned.

"What do you mean, what am I going to do?"

"Your job. You're running back and forth across the country around God knows what type of folks. You gotta take this stuff seriously." She explained.

"What are you asking me? Are you asking me if I'm going to quit my job? The world cannot stop because of this. I still have kids to take care of." I said.

"The world is going to bout stop. People are dropping like flies around the world and its getting bad here too." She pleaded.

"Look, I appreciate your concern, but we don't' live in fear."

"I'm not talking about fear. What is that job gonna do to keep you safe?" She shouted. I realized how upset she was.

"I'll call them now, and I'll let you know." I hung up the phone. We had already received updates, but at that point information was still incredibly limited. No one knew anything. All that we knew was the deadly virus was in America and the government would let us all know what was to be expected next. Granted, the same government handling the damned pandemic was currently facing an impeachment trial after Trump had the bright idea to ask the Ukrainians to investigate Biden.

Before I could call my corporate office, I heard the radio announcement that Trump had been acquitted. I took a deep breath and prepared myself for the flexing that I knew I was about to encounter as I pulled into the parking lot of another country truck stop. The first thing I saw was a rebel flag being placed near the cab of a truck that hauled logs. I drove past the truck as the driver stared at me. I felt as if he wanted me to react. I ignored him. I parked, and then headed into the store. I passed the hillbilly as he shouted.

"Woooo Hooo! Trump country baby! Trump country!!!" I entered the store as several people stood around in a circle. I looked closer.

"What's going on?" I asked.

"They're about to restock. I've been waiting all week on this" A lady said bracing herself as if she was about to run a marathon. She was anxious and almost out of breath.

"Restock? Restock what?"

"The hand sanitizer." She said as if I should have known. I looked around at all of the people. A few minutes later, this man who was shaped like a bell pepper walked from the rear of the store.

"Alright. Here we go! Here we go! I've got your sanitizer, and this is the only sanitizer you will find in Dekalb County." He explained. He held the small bottle in the air. The bottle couldn't have been but perhaps four ounces.

"Nineteen ninety-nine!" He said as he poured the box of bottles into a tub in the middle of the crowd. Immediately, the crowd began reaching and fighting for the bottles. "Look at 'em go". The man laughed. The people pushed and shoved one another. He looked at me.

"Twenty dollars?"

"Nineteen ninety-nine." He said.

"You know that price gauging is illegal." I said.

"Son, I'm just running a business. This is supply and demand." We watched as people began applying the sanitizer to their hands before they could even pay for them. He was loving every minute of it. "You better jump in there before they grab 'em all." He said to me.

"Sir, I will kick my own ass if I pay twenty dollars for that bottle of sanitizer." I said as I made my way to the drink cooler. I purchased a bottle water and returned to my truck. I didn't want to admit it, but I was growing increasingly concerned of the virus.

"VonEric, we're monitoring everything. As of right now we don't know any more than you know." My company representative informed me. "You're in that truck most of the time, so you guys may just be safer than the rest of us." She said before hanging up the phone. I texted Elijah and a few others just to check in. I fell asleep and by the time I woke up the sun was gone. I knew what that meant. It was time for the Georgian Lot Lizards to appear, and you haven't seen Lot Lizards until you've seen Georgia's Lot Lizards.

It was like watching a movie just looking out of my front windshield. Like clockwork, Lucy made her way from around the truck stop. I had seen her every time I stopped at this particular truck stop. She was perhaps sixty years old, and the con artist who ran the truck stop likely didn't care. In fact, I believe that he thought Lucy was good for business.

She wore a grey, Crimson Tide sweatshirt and a short skirt. I wondered if she were from Alabama. She waved at me as she passed by my truck. I waved back. She never offered herself to me, and I'm glad. She introduced herself once the year before as I ordered food.

"It's something about you kid. You're not like these other men. You remind me of my son, Ray." She would always say. Before long she started calling me Ray. I lost the energy or care to correct her, so I just started answering to Ray.

"Why the hell does Lucy keep calling you Ray?" One trucker one asked me as he read my name on my shirt.

"She says I remind her of her son." I explained.

"Lucy is white. Is her son colored too?" The man asked me.

"I don't know. I'm not colored either. I'm black." I said. He twisted his lip and scurried away. So, Lucy would often just wave to me whenever she saw my truck. I prayed for her safety. She knocked on my door. I rolled down my window and looked down to her.

"What's up, Lucy?"

"Here. I wanted to give you something." She said reaching into her purse.

"Lucy, I'm good. I don't need anything."

"Ray, now I ain't gone fuss with you about this. She said rumbling through her purse.

"Lucy, I'm fine. I don't need…"

"Stop it. Now, I ain't finna go back and forth with you about this. These folks is getting sick out here and you need to protect yourself. Folks is dying! This aint no joke!" She extended her hand to me as she held a bottle of hand sanitizer. I looked into her weak eyes. "Take it. Dammit Ray, Take it." She said.

I opened the door and accepted the sanitizer. I watched as a beam of joy appeared in her eyes just by the acceptance of her gift.

"I saw you standing in line in there to get a bottle. Somebody's always watching out for us." She said. Her smile faded and she limped away as it began to rain.

I knew that Lucy wrestled with perhaps cocaine addiction and mental illness, but the truckers who loved the Lot Lizards didn't care and neither did the owner of the truck stop. She climbed into the truck with the rebel flag on it. I watched the truck and a few minutes later she climbed down, stuffed her cash into her bra and walked away from the truck. Lucy walked to a puddle of muddy water in the middle of the parking lot. She stared at the puddle.

She knelt, cupped her hands together, and picked up a handful of muddy, oily, water. I cringed as I hoped she was not about to drink the water. Instead, she squatted and splashed the water between her legs. She repeated over and over again before pulling a piece of cloth from her purse and drying herself with. My heart ached. How in the fuck does something like this happen? Who was Lucy? What was her real name? Where was her family? Who was Ray? I became annoyed. Another older gentleman shut off his engine. I rolled down my window to listen as I watched Lucy near his truck. She started with the typical line.

"You want some company?" She asked. The old man looked down to her. He looked like Santa Claus. Lord, please don't let Lucy fuck Santa. I thought.

"Sure, Hun. I'd love some company. You want a bite to eat? Come join me for some dinner." He said as he prepared to leave his truck. That was nice. I thought, but that was not what Lucy wanted or needed.

"No," She said. "I mean do you want some company in there." She explained. He looked at her as if he just realized what she was offering.

"Oh. Nah, Sweetie. I don't let nobody in my truck with me. You can join me for dinner on me, but that's it."

"I don't want no mother fucking dinner you fat fuck." Lucy screamed. The man looked at her from his window. "I don't want no dinner. I'm asking you do you want to get your cock sucked or do you want to grab my tits or something, but I ain't interested in watching your fat ass eat no fucking pork chop sandwich." My heart raced. The man leaned into the truck and extended his hand out of the window.

Truckers are often in their trucks for many hours at a time, and some truckers carry what they call a piss bottle. I don't think you need much more explanation than that. I watched as the man turned his piss bottle upside down as it emptied on Lucy's head.

She screamed and screamed. I jumped down from my truck.

"Lucy!" I shouted. She was hysterical as she raced towards the store. The man made eye contact with me. I went to the store to find Lucy. I assumed she was in the ladies' room, but she never returned. By the time I went outside I saw her pointing her finger at the man while policemen stood next to her. A few minutes later Lucy was brutally handcuffed and shoved into the back of the police car.

The car drove pass me. Lucy pressed her face against the window as she looked at me. She seemed to stop smiling and almost be at peace when she saw me. I pulled my ringing phone from my pocket.

"Yea?" I answered.

"VonEric, they're shutting down." Gary, another driver said panicking.

"What? Who? Shutting what down?"

"The government. Everything. They're shutting it all down. I just lost my job."

# CHAPTER SIX

*Somethings Never Change*

I thought of Lucy constantly for a few days after I left Georgia. I prayed that she was okay. I actually hoped that someone would take steps to get her the help that she needed. I wasn't sure what that help actually was, but I hoped that someone would take steps to help her.

I had encountered many people in my life who like Lucy, struggled to exist in the world. They struggled with some sort of mental issue that led to a drug or alcohol addiction, or the other way around. However, I hated that no better solution had been found for these people. Lucy reminded me of Javon. Javon was known as the town crackhead in the small-town surrounding Stone Brook Church. He would walk the streets all hours of the night and had even been known to vandalize properties. He had issues.

Many people talked about the guy that he was before his downward spiral. Many said that Javon was a smart, talented, funny, and unbelievably athletic guy. According to some of his family who were members of Stone Brook, Javon had a promising college career ahead of him, but something went wrong. Perhaps it was the same type of wrong that had gone wrong in Lucy's life. What if it was the same type of wrong that had gone wrong in my life?

What made God decide that people like Lucy or Javon would become dependent on a substance and I might just develop an anger issue or something more socially acceptable? I'm not complaining, but at the same time I'm not actually rejoicing. I'm grateful for God's grace, but I never want to be so grateful for how far He didn't let me fall that I forget to save those who He did let fall further. Something had to be done.

Some of you reading this story and taking this journey with me have no idea what it is like to be looked at like you are complete trash, scum, dirty, and unwanted. That had been my experience from blacks in the church as well as whites in the world. Yes, there; I said it. Apparently, I wasn't the only one having that same experience and it had not changed.

It was now March 2020, and aside from America trying to figure out what in the hell was happening with Coronavirus, we were trying to figure out what the fuck was going on in Brunswick, Georgia.

A few weeks had passed since Amaud Arbery had been shot while he was just out running or jogging after a white man and his son confronted him. They claimed that he fit the description of someone who had been breaking into homes in the area, so they pursued him. We all know how that story went. The district attorney of Glynn County instructed the Chief of Police to not make any arrest. So, a few protesters were popping up across the south. I realized this as I drove to Memphis.

People were distraught over such a ridiculous loss again. Government officials had begun debating if we will need to wear face masks to help fight the spread of Covid, but I was livid.

"Black folks can't even jog down the fucking street without getting shot. You think black people are gonna feel comfortable walking into a bank or grocery store with a mask on? Trayvon couldn't even wear a hoodie." I said stirring my coffee.

"Well, they're saying it may save your life." A lady said wiping the spilled coffee, sugar, and cream from the stainless-steel countertop.

"It might. I'm just saying. Do you know how hard that is gonna be for black people? Yall aint got to think about shit like that. We do. We're already viewed as a threat by just trying to buy a hot dog, now they're telling us to put on masks?"

"I get it." She said. "Well, maybe I don't get it, but it makes sense to me. I don't understand why these types of things keep happening either. My wife is a black woman and…"

"Wife?" I asked before I realized it.

"Yes, my wife." She said putting her hands on her hips.

"It's cool. Carry on." I smiled just realizing she wore a Black Lives Matter t-shirt.

"Like I was saying, my wife is a black woman, and I am concerned for her when she's out driving all night too. She's been a trucker since before we met. That's the only reason I got a job at a truck stop, so I can be encouraging to truckers. I know the lifestyle. Does that make sense?" She asked.

"Yes, it does." I assured her.

"She has seen a lot and she has lived through a lot. Now, she's not no small little French fry gal. She's about six feet seven inches tall and two hundred pounds. She has less hair on her head than you. When people see her, they don't see a black woman. They see a black man, and that scares me." She said leaving against the counter.

"What scares you so much? The fact that she's a lesbian or that she looks like a black man?"

"People aren't out here shooting lesbians like dogs in the streets, but when she gets stopped by the police, they see her as a big burly man. That scares the crap out of me. All of these killings keep happening with police and they're she is a black and working on the road. She gets stopped by the police over and over even in her truck." She explained.

"I get it. If truckers get stopped by the police, it's not the same as a normal driver; especially if the trucker is black." She looked at me. "I get it though. The police or highway patrol stop us in their small vehicles, and they approach our semi-trucks that sit three or four feet higher than them. Then they have to look up at us and hope for our compliance when they actually know that there is nothing they can do to stop that big ass truck if we run. But that doesn't give them the right to show up at our driver's door with aggression and fear as if they're being threatened.

"You're right."

"People have got to stop being so fucking scared of things. Black people are scared of being shot, but we're not out here letting that fear control us. Those people who are marching for the jogger who was killed are afraid too!" By this time, my head began to ache. I ended the conversation and walked from the store. I headed towards my truck. I climbed into the truck and leaned my head back on the seat. Then the knocking on my door began. I looked down. There stood a woman in platinum blonde hair, leopard print tights, and a big pink feathered boa.

"What the fuck? Is this a joke?" I asked myself. She motioned her hand for me to roll down my window. I just stared at that fool for a minute until I realized that she was not going to leave. I rolled my eyes as I rolled down the window. "Mmmm Hummmm" I said.

"Hey Big Daddy."

"That's not my name woman." I said.

"Why don't you let me come up there with you and you tell me your name? My name is Bambi?"

"Bambi? Like the deer? Ma'am, please leave me alone. I'm just trying to eat my sardines and crackers in peace. Please leave me alone."

"I got something for you to eat."

"MA'AM! MA'AM, now I'm trying to be nice to you. Get the hell on now. I ain't in the mood to be dealing with this foolishness today."

"Well, I'm in the mood. I'm all the way in the mood." She said twerking on the front driver's tire.

"Lord, have mercy." I mumbled as I exhaled. "Ma'am, please don't do that. Ma'am, please don't put your ass on my wheels."

"I can make you feel good." She said shimmying.

"I can make myself feel good. Just as soon as I eat this food and go to sleep, I'm gonna feel good."

"Please. Let me come up there! You know you want to." She pleaded over and over. I realized that the woman who called herself a damn deer wasn't going to give up. I exhaled and looked around. I looked back down to her and she smiled.

"Hurry up." I said. She leaped for joy and raced around to the passenger's door as I unlocked the door. I opened it and a few seconds later Bambi climbed into the truck. She closed the door behind her. I immediately coughed.

"What the fuck did you do, eat the bottle of *White Diamonds*? You're supposed to spray a mist in the air and walk into that shit." I rolled down the windows and fanned. She looked around the truck and glanced at the bunks.

"I like to fuck on the top bunk. I give blow jobs for fifty and you can put it in for fifty-five." She said. I began to laugh. She looked at me. Then I laughed again.

"You mean to tell me for five dollars more I can put it in?" I asked as tears raced down my face while I laughed. Her smile began to fade, but I couldn't control myself. The damn crackers fell out of my mouth; I was laughing so hard. "Five extra dollars." I cried.

"Do you want it or not?" She yelled. I calmed and stopped laughing. I turned and looked at Bambi.

"Look, I don't know what your name is, but it's not Bambi. It's Detective, Officer, or Sergeant." She looked at me.

"We can do it for forty dollars!"

"Ma'am, next time you decide you're gonna try and entrap someone, don't set up your sting operation across the street from the place you're gonna hit." I laughed. She became annoyed. "I saw yall setting up across the street a couple hours ago when I first pulled into the truck stop. You look like a cartoon character. Every trucker out here knows that no Lot Lizards dress like that." I laughed. She grabbed her purse and reached for the door handle.

"Have a good night." She said in a completely different voice. She opened the door and jumped down. By the time she was back in view, she had removed her wig, heels, and the boa as she walked back towards the undercover van and SUV parked in the gravel lot across the street.

"Five dollars more." I laughed. I continued laughing as I realized it had been such a long time since I had laughed so much.

I looked around as I realized how conscious or paranoid as a black man I had become over watching my surroundings. My smile faded as I watched *Bambi* sit in the SUV. A car sped past the SUV and a few seconds later the blue lights appeared, and the pursuit began. I wondered how I was able to mock or almost laugh in the face of an undercover officer while I knew that other blacks were living in absolute fear. What if this situation had gone a completely different way? What if any other black man had accepted Bambi's offer, but then became angry when she announced she was a cop?

I wasn't the only trucker in the lot, but she didn't approach anyone else. She came for me. She waited on me. My smile was gone. I started the engine. You see, this moment had a great impact on me because it took me back to one of the most difficult moments of my life that I had ever experienced. I had not thought of the moment in so long, but the anger, hurt, embarrassment, and frustration that I experienced showed it's head that night in the truck stop parking lot.

Earl, had always been my best friend. He still is my best friend today. After thirty years of friendship, we experienced many highs and lows together. We both even began preaching around the same time during our late teens. We were serious about God, but we still liked to find outings for fun. Being that the options were limited for two young preachers, we just pretty much strolled the mall or football games.

One particular night after leaving a game at our former high school we pulled into the parking lot of a McDonalds where young people would just gather and eat. Instead of pulling into the parking space, Earl backed his Cadillac into the parking space. Earl was not at all flashy, and neither one of us cared about fancy or expensive cars or such. However, Earl's family put him in a Cadillac with chrome rims on it.

With the engine still running, I informed Earl of the recent information I had come across to getting my GED. He listened to me as a police car suddenly stopped in front of the car. Out stepped a tall black police officer. We watched as he lifted the driver's side windshield wiper and placed a parking citation under it. He then looked Earl in the eye and turned to walk away.

Earl quickly stood from the car and pulled the ticket from beneath the wiper.

"Sir, what's this? Did I do something?" Earl asked. Officer Johnson continued walking back to his car without looking at Earl.

"It's against the law to back into parking spaces in Muscle Shoals." He said. By this time, I had stepped out of the car.

"Is that a thing?" Earl asked me. I shrugged.

"Officer, I didn't know. I never heard of that." The officer returned to his car and drove away.

"It's a parking ticket for five dollars." Earl said.

"Five dollars? He could have just told you to pull in the parking space." I said.

"It's this car." Earl said shaking his head. We walked into the crowded restaurant. We stood in line. I knew Earl was pissed off, so I decided to change the subject back to my classes. The line was moving slowly. Earl continued listening and then in walked Officer Johnson again. He stared at Earl. He made his way closer to us.

"Man, just ignore him." I said softly to Earl. I then felt Officer Johnson's breath on the back of my neck. He stood with his hands on his hip as he continued staring at Earl. I continued talking, but my heart was starting to race. Kids began to notice the intense look he was giving Earl. He almost didn't blink as he stared at Earl. I continued. "So, I can the GED classes at Shoals and be done, but then…"

"Is there a reason why you are staring at me?" Earl interrupted me. I stood to the side.

"You got a problem with me staring at you?" The officer responded. Earl didn't respond. "Yea you got a problem. You've had a problem ever since I gave you that ticket."

"This five dollar ticket?" Earl asked. "I don't have a problem with a five dollar ticket sir. My problem is that you saw me still in the car. You could have just told me to reverse the car or addressed me."

"I don't have to do shit like you want. I do what the fuck I want to do." He said."

"Whoaaa, you can't talk to us like that!" I said.

"You shut up! You ain't even got your GED. You ain't smart enough to speak to me." He snapped. Earl and I were speechless, furious, and just blown away as was everyone else watching. Earl looked at me. He walked closer to me.

"Don't lose it. Turn around. We're going to order our food and sit down and eat like everyone else."

"Earl, let's just go." I said. I was humiliated.

"No. I don't trust him. He'll follow us if we leave. Just order your food." Earl said. We turned to order. Earl reached in his pocket to call his parents on his new phone. There was no answer. Officer Johnson stood over my shoulder as I ordered, he followed me to the drink machine to fix my drink, and then he stood over our booth as we ate. We continued trying to ignore him, but we could not even stand. If we stood, we would have bumped him. I felt my body shaking. I had never been so angry. I watched as Earl's hand trembled while he held his burger.

"I need a refill". Earl said. We were trapped in the booth. We both looked up at Officer Johnson. "Can you please let me out?" Earl asked. The man refused to move. Earl looked back at me.

"I want both of yall out of this restaurant! Get out now before I haul both yall black asses to jail!" He shouted.

"On what charge?" I asked. The tall man leaned over to me.

"Whatever charge I think of. They'll believe me." He smirked and I lost it. I jumped from the table.

"Earl, I can't fucking do this. Let's go!" I shouted.

"VonEric!" Earl shouted as Officer Johnson put his hand on his gun. The restaurant was silent. The entire restaurant froze. Earl's phone began to ring. His hand trembled so much that he struggled to hold it. He answered but was unable to speak.

"Mama…Mama….." His voice just faded and faded away. I could hear his mother's voice getting louder and louder as she asked him what was wrong. Officer Johnson heard her as well. He removed his hand from his holster and walked from the restaurant.

Friends, classmates, and people we knew from church all stood watching us. We left our food on the table and left the restaurant. Earl stayed on the phone with his parents while he drove me home. I felt as if I couldn't breathe.

Two days later, Earl's parents had made a complaint to the Muscle Shoals Police Department. The chief of police informed them that Officer Johnson is employed by the local managing office of McDonalds on Friday nights to provide security. The complaint was not his department's problem to handle. So, we met with a room full of McDonalds representatives, including the manager on duty that night. We met in a large conference room. In walked Officer Johnson. He spoke politely to everyone as he entered. Earl and I struggled to explain what had happened. We were both absolutely traumatized.

The district manager instructed Officer Johnson to apologize.

"If I made you boys feel uncomfortable, I'm sorry. I was just doing my job."

"That's it?" I asked.

"That's it?" Earl repeated. "We are ministers. I had just preached an entire revival to some of the same people in that restaurant, and he treated us like criminals! Thugs!" The district manager spoke.

"Well, isn't forgiveness the Christian thing to do? If you're a minister, shouldn't you forgive someone and let it go?" She patronized us. She mocked us.

"Yes." Earl's father said. He was our pastor. Earl looked at me as if he felt betrayed. I couldn't stay in that room any longer. I walked outside. A few minutes later Earl came outside to check on me.

"You good?" He asked.

"I can't believe they're just going to let him get away with what he did. Christians? What the fuck does that mean? He gets off free just because we love God? I thought he was going to shoot me!" I shouted.

"We're gonna be better for this. Both of us will be better for this. I don't know how or when, but this will be something that helps us help somebody else. Fuck him. You hear me? Fuck him." Earl said.

"They used God against us; to control us." I said. "That won't happen again, Earl. That shit won't ever happen again."

# CHAPTER SEVEN

*Not in the Mood*

Much like the rest of the workforce in America, trucking companies didn't know what to anticipate as a result of Covid-19 either. This was something that no one could have anticipated, perhaps.

Before long, Trump declared a national emergency in response to the growing outbreak. States were on strict lockdowns and every workforce was hit severely hard. Trucking decreased for most fleet companies. But after weeks turned into months, companies began to struggle. Like Gary, truckers were losing their jobs.

As I spoke to fellow truckers from various companies, I was informed that it was not so much of them getting fired. However, the workloads were decreasing so drastically that the truckers had to make decisions to leave the industry to find more stable employment.

Unfortunately, it was looking like there were no more stable workforces; at least not until the government got their hands on the virus.

"Nice day out here- it is." A fellow driver said to me as I sat on a picnic table at a rest area in Minnesota. I looked around to see the man who struggled to properly put his sentence together.

"Yes sir. It is a nice day." I said looking at all the empty picnic tables in the rest area. I exhaled. I was a little frustrated. I wasn't in a friendly mood, and something told me the moment he about fell climbing down from his truck that he was going to make his way over to me.

"You don't mind me standing next to you, do you? I know that virus got folks scared to be around one another." He laughed.

"No, you're fine." I said. I wondered why I told him that when I really wanted to tell him that I'm not in the mood to be friendly. Leave me the hell alone. I admit. I was in a bad mood. While I didn't get many calls from back home, most of the calls I did receive were negative and had something to do with someone wanting money. I tried to change my mood. I spoke.

"Yea, the news is reporting more and more cases every day. It's getting bad."

"Yes, it is, and I don't understand for the life of me why some folks don't think it's real."

"Trump told them it wasn't real." It was like the damn words just fell from my lips. He was quiet and seemed disappointed.

"You know, I think he has made mistakes, but I got faith in good ole Trump figuring this one out." I didn't reply. I was so accustomed to keeping my political beliefs separate from my workspace that I just looked at him. He made eye contact with me. "He's gonna figure out how to get folks through this." The man said drinking a can of soda. He shook his head.

"Well, my faith is in God." I said.

"Aint nothing wrong with that too. Ain't nothing wrong with that at all. But you gotta understand this one thing." He said before he stopped speaking. He looked as if he had just stopped himself from saying something that he was uncertain how I would respond.

I hoped he would stop speaking about Trump. I did not want to hear about Trump, the virus, Kobe, job loss, or any of that shit.

I just wanted some quiet time. Had I known that simply saying hello to this man would lead to a full-blown conversation, I probably would have pretended to be on my phone. I don't like being rude. In fact, I actually like making people feel comfortable, happy, and relaxed in my company. I tolerated him. I watched him struggle to balance the cigar in his mouth, Pepsi, cell phone, and bag of chips. He inhaled deeply and exhaled. Then I realized that was no Pepsi in his soda can. He looked around and grunted. Please don't sit your big ass down on this bench, I thought. You know damn well you're too big for this bench.

Then the heavy man pulled his pants up a bit and sat on the bench as I continued sitting on the tabletop. I braced myself as the bench nearly toppled and I thought I was gonna be tossed across the damn parking lot. He acted as if nothing had happened and after I was no longer angry, I then had the pressure of hiding my laugh. He spoke.

"My old lady has that virus now." He said as he stared towards the interstate.

"I'm sorry to hear that. Is she okay?"

"Well, you know them doctors. They always make things sound worse than what it is to get a couple more bucks out of you. My daughter Grace called me and told me that they have her on the ventilator. "

"Are you on your way home?" I asked looking at the truck he had walked from.

"Well, we ain't allowed in the hospital to see her, and if I turn down this here load I ain't got no guarantee my fleet leader is gonna have another load for me after my wife gets better. The only reason they still keeping me aboard is I've been with this company for ten years."

"That's more of a reason for them to assure you that your job will be safe once you get back home." I told him.

"I see who you drive for. Son, everybody ain't like that. I work for a smaller company that was handed over to the boss's snot nose ass son after he died of Covid in February. He's already changing everything.

I'm pushing seventy and I can't give them another reason to toss my fat ass on out the door." He said constantly checking his flip phone.

"Sir, if I could, I would cover your load for you so that you could go be with your wife. Even if you can't actually be inside the hospital with her." He turned to me and smiled.

"That's one of the nicest things I've heard people say in a long time." He said before getting quiet. I knew that he was deeply worried.

"It must be a little bit scary to go back and not know exactly what you're going back home to." I suggested. He nodded. I still sat on the tabletop as he sat on the bench. His shoulders moved in a way that made me wonder if he was crying.

"Corona just messes all with your breathing and stuff and she already got COPD. She don't need this damn virus. She been hauling around an oxygen tank behind her for the last year and now this. Dammit." He said. He threw his cigar to the grass and stomped on it over and over. He then buried his face in his hands.

"Did your wife smoke before she was diagnosed with COPD? I asked.

"No, I did. I done smoked a cigarette or cigar every day since I was twelve years old, and she been right there beside me since we were kids and I started smoking. Keg, them things are gonna be the death of you. She used to say as she'd fan her hand back and forth across her face. It wasn't fair then when she got diagnosed with COPD and it aint fair now that she's been diagnosed with Corona. It should have been me. She ain't never smoked one; not one!" He said. My heart ached for him.

I realized that Keg, as I assumed was his name, feared going home not just because he feared losing his job. He feared his guilt. His wife had spent a number of years ill from the side effects of secondhand smoke from him and now she battled the deadly Covid-19. I didn't know what to say to him. I was a smoker as well, but I had been on a journey to improve my physical health just as much as my spiritual health. I couldn't imagine what he might be feeling.

Truth be told, I was not in the mood to serve someone at that moment. I wasn't. I didn't feel up to it. I felt drained, and a little frustrated that someone had presented themselves to me needing something that I wasn't sure I had to give to them. That's one thing people don't like to admit. We all run out of shit. I don't care how much you love God, your family, or whatever; sometimes you feel drained and just don't feel like giving.

This is where I was when the man who identified himself as Keg presented himself to me. I was drained. My back was aching. My feet were aching. My heart was aching. I was aching, and I actually needed someone to serve my soul at that time. I became annoyed, not at Keg but at the situation, or maybe even God. A calling from God enables you to do what needs to be done when it is needed even when it is not what is the easiest thing to do.

"You have to just keep praying, and don't blame yourself. That isn't going to help you or her in this situation."

"Yea, well if them damn Democrats hadn't of had Trump all stressed out and preoccupied with this damn impeachment bullshit, then he would have been able to do right by us when it came to this virus. Now look at us." Keg deflected.

"What? What does that have to do with your wife or the people sick right now?" Keg turned to me.

"You wouldn't be stressed out if you were being lied on and dragged through court over nothing? They sabotaged him."

"Sir, first of all. I'm a truck driver just like you are. He ran to be President of the United States. He should be able to walk and chew gum at the same time. That is the biggest multi-tasking job in the world, and he shouldn't have taken it if he couldn't multi-task when things got heated." Perhaps I should have stopped speaking by that point, but I already told you that this wasn't a good day for me. "Now I understand that you're dealing with your wife's illness and you feel responsible. I understand that you're wanting to throw blame off on Trump, Democrats, congress, or even yourself; but that's not what your wife needs." I felt myself getting angry.

"Now you wait just a damn fucking minute!" He raged standing. I felt aggression and I clenched my fist. I was hoping I wasn't about to have to fight this big mother fucker, but I kind of wanted to on that day to be honest.

"No, you wait a minute. I was sitting over here minding my own business and you came to me. You need to work through your guilt or whatever it is you're feeling, but stop blaming your job, Trump, or Democrats for what you feel. You don't want to go home to see your wife because you're ashamed. Sit in that shit and own it; and then get the fuck up. Be a fucking man. Go see about your wife! Now grow the fuck up! You didn't give her COPD or Covid. She stayed next to your stupid ass all those years. It was her choice." I shouted. I was out of breath. My fingers were tingling.

We both were quiet. Can you believe that this gigantic son of a bitch started nodding and agreed?

There I was getting ready to drag him, and he agreed. He did more than agreed, he smiled.

"Ooo Weee." He said removing his cap and wiping sweat from his head. "You tell it like it is, don't you?" He said before sitting back down. I still stood there wondering what in the hell had just occurred. I looked at him as his lips began to tremble as if he was about to cry.

"She stayed with me." He said. He looked up at me and nodded again. "She stayed with me. I needed that." He said. His phone rang. Keg pulled the phone from the chest pocket of his overalls and flipped it open. He stood and began walking away as he spoke.

There I stood with sweat dripping down my face. I realized that my level of frustration that I felt before encountering Keg was not by coincidence. It was orchestrated by God and needed for my encounter with Keg. Keg needed me to be in the space that I was to reach him. My normally cool, calm, and collected self couldn't have reached him. He needed me to be at the point of knocking his ass out that I would speak freely and truthfully. As crazy as it may sound, I swear

I could feel God smiling or laughing. I need a drink. I thought.

"I'm going home!" Keg yelled from the other side of the parking lot as he still held his flip phone to his ear. "They're letting me go home." He celebrated. I nodded.

# CHAPTER EIGHT

*The Fall of America*

By April 2020, the trucking industry had lost more than 88,000 jobs. That was damn near a 5.8 percent drop from just the month before when the first shutdowns began. This was part of a record-setting 20.5 million job loss across the U.S., putting the nation's overall unemployment rate at 14.7%. What in the hell was happening?

People were stressed across the land and it could be felt everywhere. I felt it. Other truckers felt it. We all felt the stress of such uncertainty. The Centers of Disease Control had released guides for essential workers who had to continue working.

The guidance covered critical workers, such as healthcare workers, law enforcement, transportation, and logistics workers, provided they remain asymptomatic and take precautions to protect themselves and others. By this time America was masked up. We all wore masks which added to a whole new level of stress. However, we were all trying to make the best of a horrible situation. You have to understand that for so many years trucking was perhaps one of the most disrespected professional industries. No one took truckers seriously. No one really saw the value or significance in what we did, but by May the entire nation now had a new understanding.

Now most Americans had understood that Covid-19 was here, and it was not going to budge for a while. We all had to figure out what the new way of living would be and for the most part that meant something different. Social distancing required people to remain six feet from one another in public places.

Most restaurants, public places, and venues were shut down, so most people just hid out inside the house. That is what most logically thinking human beings did anyways. While there were still a group of some red hat wearing folks who didn't believe the virus was real, the majority of people opted to find new ways of life. For the trucking companies that survived the first quarter of the pandemic, they likely thrived after that once the country realized delivery and transport systems were our only way of survival. Even as talks of vaccines began to occur, who do you think would distribute the vaccines across the country? It would be the trucking companies. So, dammit, they needed to do whatever they needed to do to keep trucks rolling, because we were the most essential of essential workers.

I was happy to have consistent work. I was more than happy. I was blessed. Yes, I was blessed, and I knew it. I wanted God to know that I knew how blessed I was also. I was regularly calling home to check on my family and loved ones, but trips back home pretty much had to stop. There were a few times when I went home to visit that I would stay at a hotel instead of staying with family. While I was in a truck most of the time, I still did not want to catch or unknowingly spread the virus.

I had gotten tired of hearing all the news and mania surrounding the virus, its death toll, and the murder of Amaud Arbery. So, I stopped listening to news, media, and updates on current events. I only listened to sermons, and matters relating to spirituality. I needed to detox from all the calamity going on in the world. It was serving me well. A few weeks had passed, and I felt as if I was getting a moment to refill myself. I loved it. I had even blocked a few negative family members, friends, or people who still didn't understand that a preacher is more than just a pastor. I shut it all out and soon realized that I needed to have done that long before.

We were living with crazy levels of uncertainty. How long would the current restrictions last? When would we be able to see friends and family again? Granted, I wasn't able to see my family on a regular anyways, but the idea that I couldn't even if I were able to, was stressful.

Will the economy recover? How would we keep ourselves and our loved ones safe? When uncertainty is high, it can cause anxiety. One way people have always tried to cope with anxiety is by seeking as much information as possible.

Our foolish brains crave certainty in order to feel more in control of our lives. For example, many of us feel like it would have been easier to cope if we just knew when the COVID-19 pandemic would be over. On top of the urge to stay informed, most folks had their normal routines completely disrupted and had more time than usual to watch or read the news.

When people try to feel more in control of their lives by seeking certainty during an uncertain time, it actually makes their anxiety worse. Watching the news throughout the day or repeatedly checking social media pages for the latest updates may be comforting in the moment because it feels like we are taking steps to remain informed, which in turn reduces our anxiety. But that doesn't last long; hell, if it even works at all.

Staying glued to the news actually increases our anxiety in the long-term because it contributes to the false belief that if we have enough information, we can remain in control. In other words, the more we seek certainty over what will happen in the future, the more anxious we will feel because it is simply not possible to be certain about how long the current coronavirus crisis will last, what the world will look like afterwards, and so on. Well, I was tired of this and thankfully God showed me otherwise because I could have gone crazy just listening to everything happening. I gave myself a break, and just as soon as I gave myself the break, the crumble of America began.

On May 25$^{th}$, George Floyd died in Minneapolis after a police officer knelt on his neck for nine minutes until he stopped breathing. The video had been sent to me by dozens and dozens of truckers, truck stop workers, and people I had encountered on the road. I was devastated after watching the video and hearing this 46-year-old black man cry for his mother and plead, "I can't breathe" as he was murdered. From the moment that I saw the video I knew that this would not just be another killing of an unarmed black man. My soul shivered and I knew that shit was about to get real.

There is a moment when every black person knows that another black person is about to fucking snap. Whether it is in a grocery store, basketball game, or even at church; black people know when the line has been fully crossed. We don't even have to know one another, but we know that moment. I knew from the moment that I saw the murder that things were about to get very ugly. My first thoughts were not to call some of the people who had sent the video to me. My first thought was Elijah. While Elijah is not my only son, he is my oldest and teen son. He is in the age group of the black males that white policemen tend to believe are a threat. I could no longer go without this conversation, but I was angry. I was fucking angry.

I should not have to rip my son out of his fucking childhood innocence to teach him a lesson on how to be black around white policemen! I shouldn't have to do that to him, and it pissed me off that I did have to have this conversation. I was angry! I hid my anger as a father. I hid my anger as a black man. I hid my fucking pain. That shit hurt, but I had to talk to my son about the threat people see when they see his skin. He informed me that white police officers in Florence are friendly to him. He informed me of multiple basketball games he'd played with police officers at a local basketball court. Did that give me relief? Yes, of course.

However, you have to get this. I knew what that was, or I suspected what it could have been. Were they friendly to my son because they didn't see him as a threat, or were they friendly to Elijah because he was a star athlete at the local high school? What if he wasn't a basketball star? What if he hadn't been labeled acceptable by high school leaders? Would he still be viewed as safe? I pray that I had the conversation with Elijah without scaring him, but while still informing him of the realness of the black experience. I got off of the phone feeling stressed. I wasn't stressed at Elijah. I actually wanted to see all of my kids. Every time a black man was murdered like a dog in the streets, I wanted to gather all of my kids near me. Now, you may be wondering why Elijah is the only child I've named. It is because Elijah is older and of age to consent to me speaking of him.

People don't understand what black fatherhood is and what it means to try and be Superman in a country that has Kryptonite around every corner. Not to mention that many black men felt America had just put Lex Luther in the fucking White House.

This should not have happened to George Floyd and the fact that it could still be defended infuriated people, not just blacks.

By the next day, the Minneapolis police chief had fired all four men involved in the arrest of George. He also called for an F.B.I. investigation after the video showed that the official police version of the story was not at all accurate to what really occurred. Who didn't already know this?

That night, hundreds of protesters flooded into the Minneapolis streets. Some folks vandalized police vehicles with graffiti and targeted the precinct house where the four officers had been assigned. Officers used tear gas and fired rubber bullets into crowds. Some businesses, including restaurants and an auto-parts store, were set on fire.

Protesters began hitting the streets in other cities. In Memphis, a protest over the deaths of Mr. Floyd, Breonna Taylor in Louisville, Ky., and Ahmaud Arbery in Brunswick, Ga., led the police to temporarily shut down a portion of a street. There I was trying to then figure out who the hell Breonna Taylor was. It was all happening so fast that I couldn't keep it all straight, but I would have to brace myself to drive through it all.

In Los Angeles, hundreds of protesters converged in the city's downtown area to march around the Civic Center. A group of demonstrators broke off from the march and blocked the Route 101 freeway. Truckers were losing it.

In St. Louis, a man was killed after protesters blocked Interstate 44, set fires and tried to loot a FedEx truck. In Chicago, six people were shot and one was killed that night. The moment the FedEx truck was attacked, the trucking industry began to further panic. Truckers were breaking their company policies and carrying firearms with them for protection. Trucks were being stopped and people were climbing onto the trucks in the middle of the interstates.

The media kept insisting that the protestors were burning the cities to the ground, but there was a difference between those peacefully protesting and those who came for blood. But getting certain people to see the difference was pointless. We wondered if we were safe. Blood spilled on the road, streets, and highways as we locked our doors and continued driving.

"Hello?" I answered my phone.

"VonEric! Where are you? I've been calling you." My cousin RJ said loudly.

"I've had my phone on silent. What's up?"

"Where are you?" He repeated.

"I'm in Cleveland. Why?"

"He's in Cleveland." He repeated. I heard the commotion in the background calm. "Are they doing it in Cleveland too?" He asked someone in the background.

"Cuz, what's wrong? Is who doing what?" I asked nervously.

"You ain't seen the news?" He asked. Here we go. I thought.

"What now I asked?" Before I could respond a slew of text messages came through on my phone. I looked down to the phone on the passenger seat. Something wasn't right. A heard a voice coming through on the CB radio. "Cuz, I'm gonna call you back." I ended the call and turned up the radio.

Truckers were losing it. I struggled to make out exactly what they were panicking over. Something was wrong and my soul felt it.

"They're all over the highway." A voice said through the radio. Before I could process what was happening my phone rang. I saw my fleet leader's name pop up on the screen. I pressed the answer button on the Bluetooth.

"Hello."

"VonEric, the protests in Cleveland have turned violent. They're rioting." I didn't reply. I began looking out of my window from the interstate and sure enough massive crowds began coming into view. "You there?"

"Yea, I'm here. What do I do?" I asked as I saw the large crowds of people. I saw cars on fire. I tightened my hands on the steering wheel. Matthew spoke.

"Its just a truck, and that trailer is just a load." He said. His voice lowered. "It's not worth your life. If they want it, let them have it."

# CHAPTER NINE

*The Hitchhiker*

I appreciated Matthew's words. I really did. But to be honest, he didn't have to tell me that. Had the rioters made an effort to overtake my truck, I would have been the most compliant victim of truckjacking in history. I would have given them everything in that truck. I love my job, but I love myself more.

I made my way through the mania of Cleveland. I avoided stopping at a few truck stops I had stopped at dozens of times before because I wanted to get as far away from city limits as possible. So, I stopped at a small rest area. I was exhausted, not from the driving, but the day. I was mentally and physically drained. I decided to take a few hours to rest and sleep. That is what I did. I was awakened a couple hours later by voices on the CB radio.

"They should run over every nigger on the road." I heard. I quickly shut of the radio and returned to the bottom bunk. I couldn't go back to sleep. Eventually, I returned to the driver's seat, started the engine, and began backing up. Apparently, I went beyond the asphalt because I felt the weight of the truck shift and it slid into the muddy grass. After fifteen minutes or so of trying to get the truck free, I decided that I did not want to waste anymore time. I had a deadline to meet and the time I napped was already cutting it close. So, I requested a tow truck. I waited, waited, and waited until a large tow truck arrived. The truck backed up to my semi. I jumped out to greet the driver.

I waited for him to step from his truck. I stood outside his truck for fifteen minutes while I waited for him to address me. He finally opened his door, and stepped out as he adjusted his *Make America Great Again* cap on his head. I felt nervous the moment I saw the cap, but I checked myself. It's just a fucking cap. He doesn't deserve to be judged by that cap. I had to remind myself. I actually felt ashamed of myself. I didn't want to be wrongfully judged just because of my skin, and I almost allowed the media to cause me to judge him by his hat.

"I sure do appreciate you coming to my rescue. I'm VonEric." I said extending my hand to him. He walked past me without looking at me. He walked to the rear of the truck. He answered his ringing phone.

"Hello? Yea, I'm here. Just some ole' boy who dun got his truck stuck in the fucking mud. I swear they let any god damn fool drive these things these days." He said into the phone.

I became infuriated, but I said nothing. He walked past me again as he returned to his truck. He continued on his phone. "Yea I know, but I told your nanny that if any of them sons of bitches who are protesting come near the store to blow their fucking brains out. They're doing all this monkeying around over a fucking criminal!" He said. I looked around. The rest stop was now empty. "You know how to put it in neutral?" He asked. "You boy! I'm talking to you." He said pulling the phone from his ear.

I stared at him. We locked eyes. The moment went on and on. I wanted to lose it, but if he left, I would have to wait hours on another tow truck, and he knew it. I would miss my delivery. I sucked it up, climbed in the truck and put it in neutral as I held my foot on the breaks.

I started just praying to God in that moment because my thoughts were strong, and my rage was building. Within minutes, the truck was no longer stuck, and I was back on the road.

As the riots continued on, I continued driving through the ruins of burned cities and seeing the calamity of hurt America. I couldn't help but question if God had forsaken us.

During the day, hundreds of thousands of people joined largely peaceful demonstrations throughout the country, but cities reported hundreds of arrests as protesters fought with the police and some areas were looted. The National Guard was deployed in more than two dozen states to assist overwhelmed police departments, and dozens of mayors extended curfews.

Even in Philadelphia, a huge peaceful demonstration outside the city's art museum contrasted with the scene in West Philadelphia, where the police used pepper spray to run away looters.

In Atlanta, two officers were fired for "excessive use of force" against two college students. It was like the whole nation had gone crazy. No one seemed to be thinking of the virus anymore. In Minneapolis, about 200 protesters were arrested, and a man who drove a tanker truck toward a crowd was taken into police custody. So, that inspired even more hatred and threats towards large trucks that dared even enter the viewing of rioters.

Everything seemed like it was getting much worse. My phone rang often with family or friends asking me if I had my handgun on me for protection. I did not. It was not allowed by my company. Gun laws vary state to state so to try and meet all legal stipulations as truckers traveled would be impossible. I knew this.

This was a risk I knowingly accepted and no matter how much those who loved me tried to encourage me to break the rule for my own protection, I could not. I would not. I knew the risk. I had to remain vigilant. Truckers were being attacked, dragged out of their trucks. Trailers were being pried open and raided. This was not the movement of racial equality. This was much different. This was people who wanted something much different. I hated that the media depicted it all as being the same.

I had been driving nonstop straight to Oklahoma and it had been hours since I saw the last rioters. All I knew to do was drive. It was all that I could do. Emotions were through the roof and the warmth that once existed at truck stops was even different. People were afraid of saying the wrong things, so many people stopped saying anything. The truck stops became quiet. I hated it.

After a few months, the riots calmed, but the truck stops were still different. Even when I would visit familiar faces, they would speak, but it was different. Lot Lizards disappeared. I don't know if they were gone for good or what, but they were gone.

Trump had gassed protestors outside the White House so that he could take a photo in front of a church with a Bible. I was not aware of this until I happened to carry my Bible with me into the same truck stop that I had preached at shortly after I first began driving. Well, it was a very different vibe there now.

"Just because you carry that fucking thing don't means shit. Trump carries a Bible". I heard. How do you respond to that? Maybe you can think of a few responses and maybe I can think of a few also now at this moment. In that moment, I don't know if I was speechless or just didn't give a damn anymore. I just said,

"Okay." Then I left. I made a trip back home shortly after that. I stayed in a hotel even though family invited me to stay with them. I needed to be alone. They didn't understand that, but I needed peace. I learned of the dozens and dozens of people I knew that had not survived Covid-19. My heart ached.

Whenever I returned home, I was always informed of the regular gossip amongst the church community. I thought it was ridiculous and funny at times, but I didn't really care about it. I was just trying to spend as much time as I could fasting and praying. Yes, fasting. I had begun fasting while on the road. It became very important to me to be at my best in every way. Fasting helped me in so many ways.

I found it to be a stress reliever, and with Hurricane season making our rounds to the Gulf Coast uncertain, I needed as much peace as I could find. I hopped back in the truck, left Muscle Shoals and headed to Georgia. I drove and drove. I left Muscle Shoals more frustrated than ever. Let me explain why I left so soon after arriving. I had just been home for a day or so when my phone rang informing me of the need to make a donation to the campaign of a local politician.

"It's a shame what they're doing to her! It's a shame, and we can't just sit back and watch them destroy her. She is one of us." My cousin Erica said.

"She aint one of shit to me." I replied.

"VonEric! There you go!"

"What do you mean, there I go?" I asked.

"You don't care about anyone but yourself. Mrs. Rachel is out here trying to make a difference and them white folks is attacking her! They're trying to destroy her!" She went on and on.

"You don't even know this damn woman!" I said. You may recall the name Mrs. Rachel. Yes, this was the same woman who convinced me that aside from my great ACT test scores, I needed military discipline instead of higher education like my white counterparts. She was my black by chance guidance counselor who had dismissed so many black kids who came across her desk. Well, all these years later and she was running for her second term as superintendent for the county school system.

My cousin Erica may not have understood what had occurred, but I knew exactly what was happening the moment I heard about it. You see, Mrs. Rachel had never been known for being a black social activist. She had never shown up at a rally march, event, cause, or anything that the public was aware of. However, just like a typical politician, she jumped her ass up on stage at a racial equality march following the

George Floyd murder to scream and rant about the systemic racism in her school district that she faced.

I watched the video over and over as I watched the uninvited woman just take stage on her own and go into this tirade about systemic racism in her school district and even use the N-word. Oh, she's laying it on thick. I thought.

It wasn't but a few hours before the school district she oversaw was in an uproar, and frankly I agreed with them. Systemic racism? She was the systemic racism that so many black kids experienced including myself. Now because she needed votes, she used the pain of the black community to secure votes. The more the school system raged about her performance at the rally, the more she told supporters that she needed their support to fight the racism.

Mrs. Rachel had already been superintendent for four years. She was in charge! So, why did she wait until a couple months before her reelection to announce a racism problem in her district that other school officials said she had never presented to them.

There was no school board records of her addressing those concerns in any school board meetings. Other school officials raged that she identified a complaint on racism that she had never mentioned to them during her four years in leadership.

I knew what was occurring. It was happening all over. Some preachers were doing it too. People were capitalizing off of the pain and hurt of the black community for their own political, social, or monetary gain. I refused to give a dime to Mrs. Rachel's campaign. As people rallied harder for her, she asked her supporters to boycott businesses owned by those who opposed her or said things she disapproved of. Trump had done the same thing after the *Goodyear* company upset him. I was angry that someone could be so casual about shutting down someone's livelihood.

I could not rest in my home area knowing that so many people I loved were blind and foolishly led by such manipulation. I got back on the road and headed to Georgia. I let the situation about Mrs. Rachel annoy me so much that I lost track of time.

Midnight was nearing, and I needed to enter my time before twelve. Well, there was no truck stop or rest area near and I had five minutes remaining. I pulled the truck over on the side of the road and began to enter my time.

After I was finished, I exhaled away the foolishness that had upset me. I released my anger and bitterness towards Mrs. Rachel.

"Can you give me a ride?" A voice shouted. It scared me. I looked up to see a man standing in front of the truck. He made his way around to the driver's window which was near the highway. I rolled down my window. He left his bags in front of the truck.

"What?"

"Can you give me a ride to Exit 31?" He asked.

"Exit 31? That's all the way back that way. I'm going straight ahead. I'm sorry. I can't help you."

"Please!"

"Sorry, man. I can't." I rolled up the window and waited for him to remove his items from the gravel in front of the truck. It was dark out, and I really didn't want to try and put the truck in reverse.

I could not see behind me too well in that darkness. Eventually, he picked up his two backpacks and stepped to the side. I put the truck in drive and prepared to get back on the highway. Then almost within a second it happened. The passenger's door opened, he entered, and so did the gun.

# CHAPTER TEN

*Truck and Trailer*

Many things go through a person's mind when they're looking down the barrel of a gun. Some people think of all the things that they never got a chance to do. Some people think of all the things that they did that they wish they had gotten the chance to do over. Some people even think of nothing at all but the gun.

I wondered if God was pleased with me. I really wondered that in a way that I don't know if I had ever wondered it before. I was never the typical or easy voice of reason. I never dressed like anyone thought I should dress. I never said quite what anyone thought I should have said. I cuss, and I probably get angry faster than I should. But is He pleased with me? You know, that was really important to me. Not just in that moment as I stared into the eyes of a man who pointed the cold barrel of a gun to my forehead. I had always wondered if God was pleased with me. I didn't just wonder about it. I wanted Him to be pleased with me; not because I feared hell, but because I genuinely loved Him.

Churchy people use God in a way as if they're trying to scare people into the kingdom of heaven. I don't believe in that. There was never a time in my life that I didn't care if God was pleased with me.

"What do you want?" I said softly. I wasn't trying to whisper, but my breathing was so shallow, I could hardly speak. He didn't reply. Instead, he just reached out his hand. "My wallet? You want my wallet." I asked. "Okay." I reached my hand behind me.

"Don't you fucking move!" He said as he hit me across the face with the gun. The gun clicked.

"Okay! Okay!" I shouted as I held my hands to the roof of the truck. Blood entered my left eye.

"Don't fucking move." He said. His face was wet.

"Man, look. My wallet is in my back pocket. You can get it, but it aint no money in it. I don't carry cash. I don't have any cash." I explained. He looked deep into my eyes. He was just as scared. He spoke.

"Get your wallet." He said tightening his grip on the gun. I did as told. I opened the wallet.

"You see. No cash."

"That debit card. Give it to me." He said. I did as told. He took the card. He looked around as if he had no idea what he should do next. We both looked at my Bible beneath his muddy feet. He quickly moved his feet from the Bible. We locked eyes. Neither one of us spoke. He opened the door and jumped out of the truck. He ran into the woods. I locked the door. I then did what I had done my entire life after something difficult. I sucked it up, cleaned myself off, and I got back on the road.

Truck drivers were once ranked among America's unappreciated workers. Until the pandemic put the men and women who deliver the very goods and products that keep communities alive at the center of attention, no one paid any attention to the stress, anxiety, and experiences that truck drivers face on a daily basis.

It is no secret that truck driving includes isolation, uneven sleep, and forces truckers to operate a vehicle weighing upwards of 40 tons in a constant state of full focus. Consider those factors with being away from loved ones and general companionship for extended periods of time, and you have what could be a disaster on someone's mental or spiritual wellbeing.

For whatever reason, the trucking culture has a long-standing idea that drivers are tough-as-nails. The trucking industry is one of the industries that demands independence and emotional control.

The social isolation is one of the biggest factors behind the mental health issues suffered by truckers — loneliness and depression. Truck drivers are often expected to go entire weeks away from friends and family members, sleep at rest areas, truck stops, or alone in roadside motels.

When trucking companies are flexible about their rider program policies, allowing truckers to have a co-pilot or a spouse who signs off on a waiver, long-term solitude can be eliminated. This was one of the best policies that I encountered while trucking. I wasn't aware of this policy at first, but I thought it was such a considerate act. Now some trucking companies are hesitant to allow third parties in the rigs. But I have realized that companies are more likely to see less driver burnout with a rider program. They're also doing the right thing in terms of mental health. But on that night, I was grateful that I had changed my mind about inviting Elijah or anyone else I loved on the road with me. As I drove, I glanced down at my Bible that was covered with footprints. I knew that God had protected me, and He would continue to protect me.

No matter what situation I drove upon, God protected me. From the Hurricanes, riots, Covid-19 virus, and even the Nashville bombing, I always narrowly missed the disaster.

Years had passed since I surrendered to the direction in which God was calling my life. I was no longer a pastor in the church. To some, I was no longer a preacher. To others, I was no longer much of anything that could be easily understood, but I was fine with that. I was finally fine with not being easily understood by people. I realized that people might not ever fully understand me. Hell, I don't fully understand me. I don't understand why I will help those who hurt me. I don't understand why I will knowingly be kind to someone I said I will never speak to again. I don't understand why I still believe in love and the beauty of people no matter how much I've experienced.

I don't know why I still will give away every dime, item, or possession that I have to someone else if I even suspect they need it. I don't understand it. What I do understand, is that I don't have to understand it.

I always wanted to be the best version of myself for God, and you know what? I found that. It took me a while, but I found that. I was different because I was called to those who were just as different. I finally understood that I was like the truck that I drove, and my ministry was the trailer. I had to learn how to navigate them both so that I could not only deliver what the trailer contained but do it without hurting anyone.

Many times, the typical religious way of ministering is ripping people to shreds. It is running people off of the highway of life. It is demolishing people, and I didn't want to be that anymore. I wanted to be exactly who God was further developing me to be. I realized that everything that I held true for so long was inaccurate. I was always taught that those who didn't believe in God were evil or bad people.

I have now realized that atheist are some of the most caring people I have ever met, and American Christians tend to be the most violent, vindictive, judgmental, and least forgiving people imaginable.

I wanted to be among the people who needed me. The people who sold their bodies needed me. The people who'd lost their children needed me. Those who felt shame and guilt needed me. Even those who hated the skin I was in; they needed me too. I knew that I was equipped. I was in the right place. I was in the right space. I was on the highway to heaven.

The End

# SPECIAL THANKS

Special thanks to the following people who helped me on this journey of trucking: My boy since day 1 Earl AKA Meme, the ones who keep me rolling, Jon, John, Martin, the president of TCAM Eric, Shelby, Cedrick, Ty, Clayton. To the one who got me into trucking who seen more in me than I seen in myself my boy Bob from GE. To the ones who got me into the DI program Lisa and Kelly, to my family that's all way had my back Mary, Kim, Delois, Billy Jr, Billy Sr, Jimmy Sr, Jimmy Jr, Antonio, Darius, Kenyatta, Ashanda, and Precious. To all of my children Elijah, Vakarryius, Mattis, and Mykena. To my boys at Monarch who's always calling and checking on me Victor, Chris, and Blake. To my old boss Leonard who taught me good work ethics.

To my boy Jerome that got the first signed book. To my boys who keeps me laughing Lorance, and Stacy. To my boy for life Rich from West Palm

Beach. To my student s who taught me patient Terry and Bre. To my mentors who took the time to teach me all the knew about trucking Anwar and Mark. To the only pastor who still calls and check on me till this day Pastor Burge and the Everdale church family.

To the TCAM team who showed me the upmost generosity Caitlyn from Eagan and Dan from the ATL. To my fellow DI's Marcie, Joe, Glen, and Dan. To the ones who keep me on the straight and narrow from North Jackson Rose, Lauri, Ric, and Dave from Birmingham John and David from Eagan the master chef Darren who makes sure we have a home cooked meal. To my homies who have always been there Tri City Travelers for life George, Shawn, Robert, Jason ,and Leroy.

Thank you all. Much love,
VonEric Abernathy.

www.ingramcontent.com/pod-product-compliance
Lightning Source LLC
Chambersburg PA
CBHW071459080526
44587CB00014B/2153